Breaking Through the Clouds
by Marlene Burling
URLink Print and Media
book review by Kellie Haulotte

"All we had was each other, and the more we did together the more love we had for each other."

Burling shares her personal family stories and entwines them with passages from the King James Bible. Burling's husband, Autry, was a pastor, and she worked closely with him during his ministry work. They were married in 1962.

Burling not only shares about their years of ministry work, but she also shares how she was a caregiver to her parents and in-laws, her unbreakable bond with her grandson who was born with Down syndrome, her odd jobs, such as working as a substitute mail carrier to help with bills, and Autry's many years of struggling with heart-related medical issues. Autry, from 1993 to 2013, had two open heart surgeries and eighteen stents put in. He miraculously lived for twenty years, and this was after he was told by a doctor in 1993 that he would only make it for ten years more. After each personal story, Burling has a section with two Bible passages and a prayer. There is a moral offered for each situation.

Many readers will be able to relate to Burling's trials and tribulations and find her words quite inspiring. She not only recounts these stories but gives her readers religious advice on how to make it through the storms of life. Another thing that makes this book stand out is how Burling candidly shares her past diary entries. These passages give an even closer look at her family and the problems that were happening at the time. Burling explains that even in the worst kind of situation, God is in control and will help you in the end. Those who are looking for a new read in the inspirational nonfiction genre will find Burling's book to be more than adequate.

© 2024 All Rights Reserved • **The US Review of Books**

This review was written by a professional book reviewer with no guarantee that it would receive a positive rating. Some authors pay a small fee to have a book reviewed, while others do not. All reviews are approximately half summary and half criticism. The US Review of Books is dedicated to providing fair and honest coverage to all books.

US Review of Books

Breaking Through the Clouds
by Marlene Burling MainSpring Books
book review by Kat Kennedy

"There is no cloud so dark and threatening that our Almighty God cannot see us through."

In the book's preface, Burling states, "My desire for this book is to share my story and let you see how God worked in my life and how He can in yours also." What follows is the author's testimony of how God has given her the strength to face the many obstacles in her life. From having a grandchild with Down's Syndrome to her husband's death after fifty-one years of marriage to her own health issues, Burling has found courage and grace through her reliance on the promises of God to always be with his children. Though having been brought up in the church, it wasn't until the age of twenty-three that she became a Christian, having fully comprehended the magnitude of Romans 3:23: "For all have sinned and come short of the glory of God." She began to devour the Bible, wanting to learn all she could about God. "I couldn't read enough every day, and the things I learned about God not only built and strengthened my foundation of faith but was and is what keeps me going in my Christian walk, especially during those hard times."

From all Burling has learned after many years of walking in the Christian faith through devastating losses, she hopes to help others overcome life's obstacles through trust in God. Each short chapter of her book presents biblical truth, scripture, and an event from the author's life of how God helped her through some of the worst times. In each chapter, she gives readers the biblical scriptures needed to learn about God and his promises to his creation. Each chapter ends with a summary page of its most important concepts and scripture verses so readers can be assured of understanding. Concepts such as fact vs truth when discussing the Bible are fully explained so that readers can easily comprehend them: "The Bible is God's Word; but it will only remain a book of facts until we have personally believed in faith on the One who is the author. Fact – Jesus died on the cross. Truth – Jesus died for me!" Through the many storms of her life, Burling has relied on her faith in God, and she now shares that unwavering faith so that others may have a more abundant life as was promised by Christ.

Burling writes in a conversational manner that immediately builds trust between reader and writer. The work has the feel of an intimate conversation with a friend, and readers will come away feeling as if they really know the author. It is a personal testimony of what God has done in one life, but it offers readers all the tools needed to obtain the same faith as the author. Though the book is brief at under one hundred pages, it holds a great deal of information about walking the Christian life. Her stories of the loss of loved ones are heartbreaking, and nearly all will relate to the feelings of helplessness when faced with a loved one's illness. Burling shares journal entries she wrote during these times, which evoke in the reader the emotional devastation of her experiences. Yet through the hard times, she remains steadfast in her faith and shares that faith in this book as a way to lead others to God. Burling's desire to help others is evident in her writing. She shares the most difficult situations of her life and, even in the face of great loss, captures the beauty of God's promise of heaven. This small volume is an inspirational work intended to guide readers both to and in the Christian faith.

©2024 All Rights Reserved • **The US Review of Books**

This review was written by a professional book reviewer with no guarantee that it would receive a positive rating. Some authors pay a small fee to have a book reviewed, while others do not. All reviews are approximately half summary and half criticism. The US Review of Books is dedicated to providing fair and honest coverage to all books.

https://www.theusreview.com/reviews-1/Breaking-Through-the-Clouds-by-Marlene-L-Burling.html[6/3/2024 7:40:05 AM]

BREAKING THROUGH the CLOUDS

MARLENE BURLING

Breaking Through the Clouds

Copyright © 2024 by Marlene Burling. All rights reserved.

No part of this publication may be reproduced, stored in a retrieval system or transmitted in any way by any means, electronic, mechanical, photocopy, recording or otherwise without the prior permission of the author except as provided by USA copyright law.

The opinions expressed by the author are not necessarily those of URLink Print and Media.

1603 Capitol Ave., Suite 310 Cheyenne, Wyoming USA 82001
1-888-980-6523 | admin@urlinkpublishing.com

URLink Print and Media is committed to excellence in the publishing industry.

Book design copyright © 2024 by URLink Print and Media. All rights reserved.

Published in the United States of America

Library of Congress Control Number: 2024916598
ISBN 978-1-68486-864-3 (Paperback)
ISBN 978-1-68486-866-7 (Digital)

02.08.24

CONTENTS

Preface ix
Amid the Storm – There Is God 1
Our Shelter in the Storms of Life (Part 1) 8
Our Shelter in the Storms of Life (Part 2) 11
Our Shelter in the Storms of Life (Part 3) 15
Our Shelter in the Storms of Life (Part 4) 19
Down Memory Lane 24
Memories and Memorials 29
Till Death Do Us Part 32
Two Lives Became One 36
The Cloud of Sin Broken 39
God's Call Into Ministry 42
Ministry Years (Part 1) 46
Ministry Years (Part 2) 52
Ministry Years (Part 2 continued) 56
Ministry Years (Part 3) 59
Ministry Years (Part 4) 64
Care-Giving for My Dad (Part One) 67
Care-Giving for My Dad (Part Two) 74
Retirement 82
From a Dungeon to a Palace 86
Now that He's Gone 89
Care Giving – 24/7 for My In-Laws (Part 1) 94
Care Giving – 24/7 for My In-Laws (Part 2) 104
Alone—But Oh, So Not Alone 110
The Year – 2020! 117
My Desire – To Finish Well 122
About the Author 125

PREFACE

Life. Wow! You just never know what to expect, do you? Everything can be going so smoothly and suddenly you get an emergency phone call, a devastating report from a doctor, news of the death of a loved one, or dreams that are suddenly shattered for whatever reason. Lives are changed in a moment of time. Can we ever be prepared?

The Lord has blessed me with so many good things throughout my life, but He has also taken me down many paths of disappointments, pain, death, and grief. Along the way He has taught me many lessons, and He always assured me He would never fail me. He didn't necessarily take my situations away from me, but He carried me through them. We have a God who is compassionate, who knows and understands what we are going through and who is always at our side ready to comfort, heal, restore, and encourage.

My desire for this book is to share my story and let you see how God worked in my life and how He can in yours also. I have watched several loved ones as they passed into eternity (including my own husband). I have walked through grief (yes, I am still on that journey). I have suffered pain (physically), having had eight surgeries, suffered a heart attack and quadruple bypass surgery, and encountered several disappointments on life's journey.

My prayer is that God can use my experiences and what God has taught me to be of help and encouragement to those who need to **"break through the clouds"** of their lives.

AMID THE STORM – THERE IS GOD

"Ladies and Gentlemen, please fasten your seatbelts; we're in for a rough landing." That announcement from the pilot immediately sent a spine-tingling shiver up my back. Storm clouds were ahead, and as the plane began its descent it wasn't long before we were engulfed in those ominous black billows. Darkness soon engulfed us while we bounced up and down. Trying to calm my jittery nerves, I quickly prayed, "Lord, I know you are with me, and you are in control. I don't have to be afraid. So, why am I?" Immediately the Lord seemed to be saying, "How silly, after all I have just brought you through."

My thoughts were drawn to just four months prior to this flight. One day early in May of 1993, my husband began to experience chest discomfort while we were walking our usual four miles a day. (This was during our ministry in Strodes Mills, PA). He attributed it to "indigestion," until later in the month he couldn't complete a mile; and within days from that couldn't walk from one room to another without experiencing chest pain. A stress test quickly revealed my husband was ready to have a heart attack. We weren't ready to hear those piercing words. He was immediately admitted to the cardiac intensive care unit. I couldn't believe what was happening.

The clouds of reality surrounded me as I walked into our home that night--alone! "Is this what it was going to be like from now on? What if Autry would never be here again?" The next few days revealed just how serious the situation was. His main artery to the left side of his heart was 90 percent blocked. Open heart surgery was quickly scheduled.

I had known the Lord for 30 years and I knew He was in control. I knew He was with me, and yet I had never felt so alone. The reality that I might not have my mate with me much longer just made my inner being ache.

Then one evening while driving home from the hospital, my eyes were drawn like a magnet to something I'd driven by hundreds of times before but had never really noticed. Now it haunted me. There they were--monument stones! "No Lord, I don't want to think about that," I practically shouted. And yet my thoughts screamed at me, "You've got to be prepared." "Prepared?" I asked myself. "How do you prepare for something like this?" More questions raced across my mind. "If the Lord calls my husband home, where would I live? What would I do for a living? We don't have our own home. We live in a parsonage, and except for working three years as a secretary early in our marriage, I have never held a full-time job. What would I do?"

The loneliness during those long hours was overwhelming despite support from family and friends. How often I cried and poured my heart out to the Lord asking Him to spare my husband's life, to keep us together so we could continue to serve Him in the church where we had been called to just fifteen months earlier and we had come to love. We had never been happier. I believed God could make my husband well, but I also knew He is a sovereign God and if He so felt my husband's ministry was finished, He could call him home. Somewhere during those long days, I was able to pray, "Not my will, but yours be done."

The bypass surgery was successful. The doctors reported they usually didn't find that blockage in patients until it was too late, as it was located in a very dangerous location. It is called "the widow maker." We praised the Lord and felt He had performed a miracle. He had spared my husband and let me bring him home again. What a special day that was.

The healing process in a procedure such as this is long and trying, but at the same time amazing as we think of the way God has made our bodies to endure and mend. My husband seemed to be making progress--up to a point. He reached a plateau, and then actually began to regress. We soon found out why. During one of his exercises at the hospital cardiology rehab unit, the monitor recorded a problem. The phone rang. Once again, I wasn't prepared for what my husband was about to share. "They won't let me come home. They're admitting me right away. Something is wrong!" "How could this be? Why, Lord? Not again. I can't stand it! What's happening?" Questions with no answers overwhelmed my aching heart once again.

Within a few days the doctors had stabilized my husband's condition, but further tests revealed a startling situation. My husband's by-pass had failed; it was totally blocked and literally had "died off." He was back to his original condition which now had deteriorated even further. Since my husband was classified "high risk," another by-pass was ruled out; so a specialist in Atlanta, Georgia was consulted about performing a new procedure. Autry was released from our local hospital, and we waited together for the phone call bringing us news of when we were to go to Atlanta, Georgia. Finally, it came. In one week, he was to have another operation.

That week of waiting was such a growing experience for us. We cried together; we prayed together. We were afraid; yet we trusted our Lord through it all. We held each other and our love grew even deeper than we ever imagined for each other and also for our Lord. And yes, we talked about him *not being here anymore*. It was a week I'll never forget. We were both in God's hands and there we rested. We rehearsed Isa. 41:10 many times: "Fear thou not, for I am with thee, neither be afraid for I am thy God. I will strengthen you, yes, I will help you; I will uphold you with my righteous right hand."

The day to fly to Atlanta, Georgia arrived. The Lord graciously made it possible for our three children and my father-in-law to be with us. We were all flying from different parts of the country. Our family had always been close, but this was a special time as they showed their father and me how much they loved us. We checked into the hospital on a Friday morning around 9:00 am. Before they took Autry to surgery, our family stood around his bed holding hands and praying that God would direct the surgeon's hands; and would let it be a successful procedure. At 1:00 p.m. we watched as they rolled him down those silent halls and through some double doors. As the doors closed behind him, I didn't know if I'd talk to him again "in this life." My family gathered in the waiting room, and we did just that—wait. And wait. I prayed, and our children prayed as the minutes ticked away. I wondered, "How can anyone go through this without the Lord's strength and help?" I could not.

Three hours later a nurse entered the room. "Is the Burling family here?" she asked. We quickly responded. "He's doing fine. You may see him," she said. I've never heard any sweeter words. "My Autry is fine! Thank you, Lord." We soon realized what a miracle it was that Autry had even been walking around prior to surgery when the doctor informed us the main artery had been over 95% blocked with only a hair line of blood flowing through. The Lord is good! Less than 24 hours later he was released, and the following day we flew back to Pennsylvania.

The plane began to break through the black clouds. Rays of sunlight streaked through the window. The plane still bounced from the turbulence, but at last we were through; the runway was directly ahead. What a glorious sight! We were almost home; home, with my husband beside me. I could still see those billowing, frightful storm clouds towering above, but now there was also light, such a welcomed sight. The blackness of the storm clouds above us didn't appear as overwhelming once the rays of sunlight provided hope of breaking through.

Many times we are overwhelmed by storms in our lives; but no matter how black they may be, there is always hope of breaking through. The rays of God's love are always shining down upon us (even when we can't see or feel them), and through the light of His Son, Jesus Christ, there is peace.

As I read the paper, see TV news reports, and see members of our own families and churches, my heart aches for those who are surrounded by storm clouds. Many are much greater than I have experienced. People are hurting, they are crying. They are falling apart and looking for a way out, or at least a way to bear their pain.

None of us know what tomorrow may bring. It can be certain, in one form or another, storms will come. Though they may come unannounced, and come quickly, we can make some preparation ahead of time.

There have been times I thought about the "what ifs." What if my husband had gone home to be with the Lord? What if I had been left a widow? (Yes, that came years later!) What if I had to find a job, another place to live? I am confident that just as the Lord saw me through a very difficult experience, He would also have faithfully provided for any other needs I may have encountered. He will do the same for you. There is no cloud so dark and threatening that our Almighty God cannot see us through. He is always there! What kind of cloud engulfs you right now? God is there to help.

BE STILL AND.....

> Many times, we are overwhelmed by storms in our lives; but no matter how black they may be, there is always hope of breaking through. The rays of God's love are always shining down upon us even when we cannot see or feel them, and through the light of His Son, Jesus Christ, there is peace.

READ THE WORD

"Fear thou not, for I am with thee, neither be afraid for I am thy God. I will strengthen you, yes, I will help you; I will uphold you with my righteous right hand."
Isa. 41:10

HIDE THE WORD

"You will keep him in perfect peace whose mind is stayed on thee." Isa. 26:3

PRAY THE WORD

Dear Father, There are storm clouds all around me. Please help me to keep my mind stayed on you so I can have peace. Calm my fears and give me the strength I need during this time. Amen

KNOW THAT I AM GOD

Psalm 46:10

I feel that the next four sections are the most important in my book because it lays the foundation of my faith and lets you (my readers) see where my strength has come from and how I can say we can break through the clouds in our lives. It was vital in my growing in the Lord and showing me how I could trust my God and Savior with everything going on in my life. I learned who God is, what He can do, what He does do, and how much He loves me and how much He loves you.

My desire is that as you read this you will realize what an awesome God we have and that you will **know** that He will help you break through any cloud surrounding you now or that will come.

This is the God I came to love and trust and why I claimed Gal. 2:20 as my life's verse: ***"I am crucified with Christ, nevertheless I live; yet not I, but Christ lives in me, and the life which I now live in the flesh, I live by the faith of the Son of God, who loved me, and gave himself for me."***

OUR SHELTER IN THE STORMS OF LIFE

(Part 1)

Fasten your seatbelt; the flight of **L-I-F-E** is about to take off. Decisions must be made. Which plane will you board? What flight path will you travel? What will be your destination?

When I was a young girl and teenager I religiously went to church on Sunday and said my prayers at night. From my bedroom window in the farmhouse I grew up in, I would often get on my knees and look up at the glistening moon and the twinkling stars and pray to God in Heaven. Sometimes it seemed that face in the moon was actually God smiling down upon me. I loved going to church and I was active in our small youth group. We didn't take Bibles with us to church, but for our confirmation class we had to learn the Books of the Bible. Each of us was required to report on one Book. I was assigned the Book of Ruth. At the conclusion of the classes, we were made members of the church. Since I had never been baptized as a baby that was also required at that time. So, there I was, baptized by sprinkling, a member of the church and I hardly missed a Sunday service. Heaven, here I come!

Satan is going about as an angel of light in churches across our nation making people just like me feel "safe and secure," while all the time he is leading them straight to hell. It doesn't matter if you are like I was; a good little Methodist girl, or the world's most hideous murderer. We all start out aboard the plane of **D-E-A-T-H** piloted by Satan himself, with our course and destination both headed for the Lake of Fire.

But look across the runway; there's another plane. Notice the letters: **L-I-F-E**. Who's the Pilot? None other than the Wonderful Counselor, the Mighty God, the Everlasting Father, the Prince of Peace, the Lord Jesus Christ. In April of 1967 my eyes were finally opened as the Spirit of God moved in my heart. This good little Methodist girl wasn't as "good" as she thought she was. When the truth of Romans 3:23 *"For all have sinned, and come short of the glory of God",* sank into my inner being, I saw myself lost and on my way to hell. John 3:16 *"For God so loved the world that He gave his only begotten Son, that whosoever believes in him should not perish, but have everlasting life,"* and Romans 6:23 *"For the wages of sin is death, but the gift of God is everlasting life through Jesus Christ our Lord,"* gave me the hope I needed. Jesus Christ died for me! He loved me so much He was willing to die for my sins on a cruel cross. I didn't deserve it, but I believed with certainty and became His child that day as I prayed on my knees in my bedroom. This time as I prayed to the God of Heaven, He became my Heavenly Father.

I had broken through my clouds of sin through Jesus Christ, who loved me and gave himself for me and I began my journey on flight **L-I-F-E**. I was 23 when I became a child of God. I hungered to know all I could about my Pilot. The word of God became so important to me from the day I accepted Jesus as my Savior. I couldn't read enough every day, and the things I learned about God not only built and strengthened my foundation of faith but was and is what keeps me going in my Christian walk, especially during those hard times.

BE STILL AND.....

> Do you know for sure that you are on flight L-I-F-E?

READ THE WORD

"For the wages of sin is death, but the gift of God is everlasting life through Jesus Christ, our Lord."
Romans 6:23

HIDE THE WORD

"For God so loved the world that He gave his only begotten Son, that whosoever believes in him should not perish but have everlasting life."
John 3:16

PRAY THE WORD

Dear Father, I know I am a sinner and I believe that Jesus Christ died for my sins. I ask you to forgive my sins and to come into my life and be my Savior. Thank you for loving me and for saving me and giving me everlasting life. Amen.

KNOW THAT I AM GOD

Psalm 46:10

OUR SHELTER IN THE STORMS OF LIFE

(Part 2)

It's a fact--all through life we are faced with storm clouds. Some bring only showers and others are like monstrous hurricanes leaving devastation in their path. We question, "Why?" We look for answers, but we don't always find them. There is only one thing for certain. Our almighty, omniscient God allows these things in our lives; never to drive us away from Him, but to draw us closer. When storms in our lives do drive us away from God, it's because of our own volition and perhaps we are ignorant of whom this God really is and what He can do for us, in us, and through us. When storms arise, we can either fall apart at the seams, or be held together by the precious interwoven threads of God. As His children, the more we know about our God and the closer our daily walk is with Him, the more we will trust Him when the storm clouds appear. We can rest in our Lord even when there are no answers.

How Satan would love to keep us imprisoned in our clouds, but Jesus says, "Remember Me; remember my Word." In Hosea 4:6 God says, *"My people are destroyed for lack of knowledge."* Are we overwhelmed amid our clouds because of our lack of the knowledge of God? Perhaps! Paul's goal in life was, *"that I may know Him and the power of His resurrection…"* Phil. 3:10. God gives a special promise to those who know His name. *"Because he hath set his love upon me, therefore will I deliver him; I will set him on high, because he hath known my name. He shall call upon me, and I will answer him. I will be with him in trouble; I will deliver him and honor him. With long life will I satisfy him and show him my salvation. ...because he hath known my name..."* Psalm 91:14-16. Here lies the key. Without the use of names, we would be unable to relate to others. God has made Himself known to us through His names. Since we are dealing with life's storms, I am especially interested in one Name. So, let's start at the beginning.

Look at the fourth word in your Bible; *"In the beginning God..."* Gen. 1:1. What's so significant about this? Absolutely everything! The Hebrew for this first name of God is Elohim, a uni-plural noun, denoting one God who is a trinity. We can break it down like this:

El - the singular word for God – meaning the Strong One

Oh - to take an oath or covenant – meaning to swear; the Faithful One

Im - is a Hebrew plural ending – denoting the three-in-one Godhead

So, we have Elohim (the triune God), the Strong Faithful One. Notice also how it is spelled in the King James Version of the Bible, capital G, lower case o and d. It appears over 2500 times in this fashion. It is a name that is full of assurance for our faith. It is a name that can bring us comfort unlike any other name on earth. Since the name refers to the absolute, unlimited power, energy and faithfulness of God, we can be assured He is always ready to use these attributes on our behalf.

This "Strong, Faithful One" has given numerous promises, not only to men found in the scriptures, but promises He has made that each of us can claim today. He promised a Redeemer. He sent the Lord Jesus, the greatest of all His promises. And this Redeemer lives in each of us (who have received Him as Savior) in the third Person of the Trinity. **MARVELOUS!**

The Creator, God, our Elohim was powerful enough to speak into existence the universe; to breathe the breath of life into man, and to defeat Satan at the Cross. He did not create everything and just abandoned it. Col. 1:17 *"...And by Him all things consist."* The whole universe is kept by the power of our Elohim. **We** are kept by the power of Elohim. Isn't He also powerful enough to help us through our clouds and storms of life?

He was faithful to Abraham. *"...he that shall come forth out of thine own loins shall be thine heir."* Gen. 15:3. Isaac was born when all human reason said, **IMPOSSIBLE!**

As Elijah fled from the wicked rule of Ahab and Jezebel after predicting there would be no dew or rain for three years, God promised He would sustain Him. Can't you just hear it, "Spread your napkin, Elijah; here comes your supper on flight R-A-V-E-N!" Later, in the home of a widow, a barrel of meal and a cruse of oil didn't know their limitations and lasted until it was no longer needed. **INCREDIBLE!**

There was Joshua; ready to take over the leadership of a great nation after they had followed one of God's greatest servants, Moses. God said, *"As I was with Moses, so I will be with thee; I will not fail thee, nor forsake thee. Be strong and of good courage."* Joshua 1:5,6. Joshua could be strong and take courage only because his God, his Elohim, was strong and faithful to keep His Word. **INVINCIBLE!**

Mark this in your Bible: Numbers 23:19: *"God is not a man, that He should lie; neither the son of man, that he should repent. Hath He said, and shall He not do it? Or hath He spoken, and shall He not make it good?"* So, when God says:

"I will never leave thee." Heb. 13:5
"Call unto me and I will answer thee." Jer. 33:3
"My God shall supply all your need." Phil. 4:19
"I can do all things through Christ who strengthens me." Phil. 4:13
"They that wait upon the Lord shall renew their strength." Isa. 40:31
"Fear thou not, for I am with thee. Be not dismayed; for I am thy God, I will strengthen thee; yea, I will help thee; yea, I will uphold thee with the right hand of my righteousness." Isa. 41:13
"No good thing will he withhold from them that walk uprightly." Ps. 84:11
"Who (What) shall separate us from the love of Christ?........Nay, in all these things we are more than conquerors through him that loved us." Rom. 35-37.
"Casting all your care upon Him: for He careth for you." I Pet. 5:7
Does God say, "Oh! Excuse Me, I didn't really mean what I said?" Emphatically, "No!" Should you still question, reread Numbers 23:19. What a great God we have!

BE STILL AND.....

> As His children, the more we know about our God and the closer our daily walk is with Him, the more we will trust Him when these storm clouds appear.

READ THE WORD

"My people are destroyed for lack of knowledge."
Hosea 4:6

HIDE THE WORD

"God is not a man, that He should lie; neither the son of man, that he should repent. Has He said, and shall He not do it? Or has He spoken, and shall He not make it good?"
Numbers 23:19

PRAY THE WORD

Dear Father, help me to know you more, and to trust in your unlimited power and faithfulness, and to claim the precious promises You have made to me. Amen.

KNOW THAT I AM GOD

Psalm 46:10

OUR SHELTER IN THE STORMS OF LIFE

(Part 3)

As a new Christian, there were things I needed to deal with and to learn. About a week or two after I trusted the Lord Jesus Christ as my Savior, I suffered from D.D.D.S. It was "life" threatening; it was physiologically debilitating; neurologically paralyzing along with psychologically impairing! This **dis**-ease is very common in newborn Christians, and though *life threatening*, it is curable. I call it the "Devil's Devious Doubting Syndrome." The first symptom of this **dis**-ease is when you hear a voice saying, "You don't really believe you are saved and going to heaven, do you?" A second symptom may be loss of joy, causing the muscle in your mouth to constrict just when you need it the most. The third and perhaps the most "life" threatening is depression. When all of the above are present, Satan has you just where he wants you; a new-born, locked in D.D.D.S.; of little use to God and most miserable. There is only one cure. It's safe, it's simple, and it's as free as salvation itself. It's the Word of God. Do you need to break through your clouds of doubts of salvation?

Your salvation was received by faith. Romans 8:9 says: *"For by grace are ye saved through faith..."* Your victory over these clouds of doubt is received the same way. Have you forgotten the One who spoke these words of promise; our God, our Elohim; the Strong and Faithful One who is the Promise Keeper? Look what else He says in John 3:17: *"He that hath the Son hath everlasting life."* And to top it off, our salvation is a **know-so** salvation; not a hope-so salvation as I John 5:13 says: *"These things have I written unto you that believe on* the name of the Son of God; that you may **know** that you have eternal life, and that you may believe on the name of the Son of God." Also see this: Eph. 1:12-14. *"That we should be to the praise of his glory, who first trusted in Christ; in whom ye also trusted, after ye heard the word of truth, the gospel of your salvation; in whom also after ye believed, ye were **sealed** with that Holy Spirit of promise, who is the earnest of our inheritance until the redemption of the purchased possession, unto the praise of his glory."* We hear the Word. We trust in Christ for salvation, and we are sealed. Notice it's with the Holy Spirit of *promise*. Is it sinking in?

When our feelings say, "I've lost my salvation," or "I can't really be saved," we make the cross of Christ of no effect. We question the power of our Lord and Savior. We question the very Word He spoke. If Jesus was powerful enough to save us from our sin, is He not also strong enough to keep us saved? Is He not strong enough to break us through our clouds? *"Hath he not said, and shall He not do it? Or hath He not spoken, and shall He not make it good?"* Num. 23:19. Some would say this gives us a license to sin. God forbid. *"How shall we that are dead to sin, live any longer in it? ...like as Christ was raised up from the dead by the glory of the Father, even so we also should walk in newness of life."* Rom. 6:2, 4.

Romans, chapter 7, lets us know we still have our "human or fleshly" nature, and there is a battle within our members between our old and new nature. But no matter how thick the clouds of the old, they can't begin to compare to the "son-shine" of the new; and verses 24 and 25 give us the victory. *"Oh, wretched man that I am! Who shall deliver me from the body of this death? I thank God through Jesus Christ, our Lord..."*

An admonition is also given to us in I Peter 1:15, *"But as He who hath called you is holy, so be ye holy in all manner of life."* As born-again children of God this will be our desire. We will have no desire to commit sin. *"Whosoever is born of God doth not commit (practice) sin, for his seed remains in him, and he cannot (i.e. does not practice) sin, because he is born of God."* I John 3:9. (emphasis added)

John was writing to Christians in I John as he uses the words "little children." He reminds us we will have sin in our lives, but he also reminds us in verse 9 of chapter 1, *"If we confess our sin, he is faithful and just to forgive us our sins, and to cleanse us from all unrighteousness."* This is a daily cleansing. Salvation is a one-time happening, but we need to bathe daily to rid ourselves of the sins that soil our lives. As an earthly father is grieved when his child goes astray, so the Heavenly Father is grieved when His children stray. We have the privilege of going to God directly and saying, "Father, I have sinned; please forgive me."

BE STILL AND.....

> There is only one cure for the "Devil's Devious Doubting Syndrome" (D.D.D.S). It's safe, it's simple, and it's as free as salvation itself. As Your salvation was received by faith, your victory over sin and any clouds of doubt is received the same way.

READ THE WORD

"That we should be to the praise of his glory, who first trusted in Christ; in whom ye also trusted, after ye heard the word of truth, the gospel of your salvation, in whom also after ye believed, ye were **sealed** *with that Holy Spirit of promise."*
Eph. 1:12-14.

HIDE THE WORD

"Oh, wretched man that I am! Who shall deliver me from the body of this death? I thank God through Jesus Christ, our Lord..."
Rom. 7:24, 25

PRAY THE WORD

*Dear Father, I am so thankful for the day You
saved me. I ask you to forgive me
of the sins in my life right now. I am claiming
victory over them and the dark cloud
that is encompassing me right now because of the promises you have
given to me through Your word. Amen.*

KNOW THAT I AM GOD

Psalm 46:10

OUR SHELTER IN THE STORMS OF LIFE

(Part 4)

So often our "feelings" prevent us from being and enjoying all God intended for us, and blinds us to biblical fact and truth. A.W. Tozer said, "A fact may be detached, cold, impersonal and totally disassociated from life. Truth, on the other hand, is warm, living, and spiritual." He also said, "Theological facts are like the altar of Elijah on Mt. Carmel before the fire of God came—correct, properly laid out but altogether cold. When the heart makes the ultimate surrender, the fire falls and true facts are transmuted into spiritual truth that transforms, enlightens, and cleanses. At what point then, does a theological fact become for the one who holds it, a life-giving truth? ...At that point where faith and obedience begin."

Perhaps you are familiar with the words of an old chorus, "God Said It, I Believe It, and that Settles It for Me." The Bible *is* God's Word; but it will only remain a book of facts until we have personally believed in faith on the One who is the author. **Fact** - Jesus died on the cross. **Truth** - Jesus died for *me*! It's settled - not on my merits, but because of Who God is. So, to get rid of D.D.D.S., do what I did. When our **feelings** start getting in the way, go back to God's Word and read what He has to say to us. Remember, it's **truth** that we have believed in **faith** and regardless of how we *feel*, it remains truth. It's settled, not because of my feelings, but because of **Who God Is**.

A look at another portion of scripture will give us further insight into our wonderful God that will provide us with more foundational truth for us to cling to amid our clouds. You may have been taught the facts that God is omniscient, omnipresent, and omnipotent and you may have said, "What a wonderful God!" But have the facts become truth to you? As we are building more foundational truth for us to cling to amid our clouds, think about these *truths* from Psalm 139:

God knows *me*. He created everything, everyone. Yet out of all the universe, He knows *me*. vs. 1

He knows when I sleep, when I rise. vs. 2

He knows my very thoughts. vs. 2

He knows my every step I take. vs. 3

His eye and His hand are upon me. vs. 5

No matter where I go, He is with me. I cannot see Him, but He is there. Even in the thickest darkness I am not hidden from God's eye. vv. 7-10

God knew me even in my mother's womb. He made me special. vv. 13-16

"How precious also are thy thoughts unto me, O God! How great is the sum of them! If I should count them, they are more in number than the sand; when I awake, I am still with thee." vv. 17, 18

Ponder these. Memorize them, let them fill your whole being. There is nothing about us that God is not interested in. He knows our pain and our hurt. He knows we are weak, and He hears our cries. When we think there is no one who cares when we are swallowed in the darkest storms, God is there!

One other attribute of God is imperative for us to contemplate as we consider the storms in our lives. Sovereignty. One definition says, *"He (God) yields to no other power, authority or glory, and is not subject to any absolute greater than Himself."* Simply because He is God, He possesses and exercises supreme authority over all His creation, including man. God can do as He pleases.

"… according to the purpose of Him who worketh all things after the counsel of His own will." Eph. 1:11. *"But our God is in the heavens: He hath done whatsoever He hath pleased."* Psalm 115:3. Whenever you are tempted to question God's moral right to do as he pleases, read Job 38:1-40:5. You will be brought to silence as was Job.

Be assured of one other thing. God is also holy. He will never act outside of that attribute. He is never out to "get you." His desire is, *"that all things work together for good to them that love God, to them who are the called according to His purpose. For whom He did foreknow, He also did predestinate to be conformed to the image of his Son..."* Romans 8:28, 29. Yes, it is He Who brings us or allows us to enter our storms. He knows the beginning from the end and uses all our circumstances including those dark clouds to make us like His Son. Ours is not to question, but to trust.

In Psalm 37 we have yet another lesson for us. How many times have you said, "The unbelievers seem to get all the breaks; look how they are prospering?" It may appear that way; but study this Psalm carefully:

vs. 10 *"For yet a little while, and the wicked shall not be."*

vs. 13 *"The Lord shall laugh at him; for He sees that his day is coming.*

vv. 35-36 *"I have seen the wicked in great power and spreading himself like a green bay tree. Yet he passed away and, lo, he was not."*

Never envy the unbelievers. Everything is not well with them. Yes, we may suffer in this life, but what lies ahead for us in eternity as believers far outweighs any pain or inconveniences we may suffer in this life. God encourages us in this same Psalm. He says rest, wait patiently, fret not, delight in the Lord, commit your way to Him, and trust Him.

vs. 24 *"Though he falls, he shall not be utterly cast down; for the Lord upholds him with his hands."*

vs. 39 *"But the salvation of the righteous is of the Lord; He is their strength in the time of trouble."*

Is the unbeliever able to claim such hope?

In our quest to "break through the clouds," I have laid out some fundamental truths to encourage us. Please remember, we are still captives in our human bodies; there are going to be times when storm clouds rise, and we will find that answers aren't enough; or perhaps there just won't be an answer. God is still there; He always will be. God is God!

So, as we prepare to board our flight, let me ask you:

Do you have your ticket? It's free (John 3:16)
Are you sure? (I John 5:13)
Are you well acquainted with the Pilot? (II Tim. 2:15)
Then fasten your seatbelt because Flight **L-I-F-E** is about to take off!

BE STILL AND.....

> You may have been taught the facts that God is omniscient, omnipresent, and omnipotent; He is holy, and He is sovereign and you may have said, "What a wonderful God!" But have the facts become truth to you?

READ THE WORD

"And we know that all things work together for good to them that love God, to them who are the called according to His purpose. For whom He did foreknow, He also did predestinate to be conformed to the image of his Son..."
Romans 8:28, 29

HIDE THE WORD

"But the salvation of the righteous is of the Lord; He is their strength in the time of trouble."
Psalm 37:39

PRAY THE WORD

Dear Father, I realize You have allowed this dark cloud to surround me. Use it, dear Lord, to make me more like my
Savior, the Lord Jesus Christ.
And even when there is no answer, I know You are with me. Amen.

KNOW THAT I AM GOD

Psalm 46:10

DOWN MEMORY LANE

As I walked down what used to be called Cherry Lane, my eyes flooded with tears. The elegant black cherry trees that once lined the sides of the lane that led from one pasture lot to another on my father's farm were gone. The wild grapevines that had been a tapestry of green cascading from high in the nearby trees and blanketing everything beneath them I could only picture in my mind. The old apple trees stood with decaying limbs tangled and bending to the ground. I looked for my secret garden in a hollowed-out tree with rich black soil packed inside. It was gone. I saw the birch trees etched with dates and initials of old boyfriends and girlfriends surrounded by hearts. Stumbling over rocks and climbing over fallen dead tree branches, I made my way around the pasture lot. I found no "puff balls." As kids, we were fascinated by these mushroom-like plants, the size of a soccer ball, white in color until fall came. They then turned brown and when we kicked them, they would disintegrate into a puff of brown dust.

Only a few cows were gathered at the pond eyeing me as I passed by; probably wondering, "Who's this stranger?" Finding a soft, grassy spot under a tree, I sat, suspended in time, looking around and remembering how it "used to be." Our farm—it was the most wonderful place on earth. As children, we were safe, happy. We had the largest playground of anyone I knew.

It was getting late as I headed back up the lane. The old barn stood silhouetted against the graying sky. I wondered if it, too, was weeping from sagging rafters, fading color, broken windows and the silence. As I walked toward the house another lump settled in my throat. The bushes had grown uncontrollably. Only the poppies and peonies had managed to survive, but they were being crowded out with weeds. The house itself was groaning in pain. The stucco had become too heavy for the house to bear, and cracks were winding their way throughout, causing some to crash to the ground. When I walked up the cement steps and into the country kitchen, there was no smell of cookies baking. The curtains, now worn and faded, the wallpaper yellow and dusty, cobwebs hanging in the corners, all cried out that someone is missing. She's not busy baking yummy pineapple cookies or preparing meals fit for a farmer's appetite. She's not cleaning, nor is she sitting in her favorite spot by the kitchen window watching her birds playfully fly in and out of the bushes. Mom is gone. The house is silent.

Mom was 18 when she married my dad. They had grown up together as neighbors, were childhood sweethearts. She knew all about the man she was going to marry, and she chose to marry 'til death do us part. She didn't have all the luxuries of many women. Every Monday the old ringer washer and rinse tub occupied a major part of the kitchen. She knew what hard work was. She kept her husband satisfied and cared for and loved her children. The farmhouse was large with high ceilings, wallpapered throughout. Though it wasn't fancy, to us kids and Dad it was a palace with the most wonderful queen graciously adorning it with her presence. She was the most selfless person I've ever known; always putting Dad and her children's needs ahead of her own. Life wasn't easy on the farm; it took hard work, long hours, and commitment. The cows were milked twice a day regardless of weather or illness. There was no getting around that. When the fields of wheat or oats were golden yellow, they were ready to harvest; there was no time to waste. Personal needs or desires had to be put on the back burner. But Mom had made a lifetime commitment and no matter how difficult the times were, she was there to stay.

My husband had often told people that he "fell in love" with my mom before he fell in love with me. He thought, "If her daughter turns out to be like she is, that's who I want to marry!" I couldn't have had a better role model.

Super Bowl Sunday, 1989, the phone rang after our morning church service. "Mom is in the hospital! They say she has pneumonia." We didn't feel, at the time, it was necessary to head up to see her; and since we still had evening service responsibilities we waited. We hadn't been home long after that service when the phone rang once again, but this time broken words were heard, "They're calling the family in; Mom is dying!" I don't know how I did it; I was so shaken, but I threw clothes in a suitcase, even dress clothes (just in case) as did my husband. He drove (more like flew) as I sat crying most of the two-hour drive, just looking up at the moonlit sky and praying. At exactly 9:00, as I looked at some white clouds starting to cover the moon, somehow I knew, and I said, "She's gone!" We raced up flights of stairs at the hospital, not waiting for the slow elevators and as we opened the door to the waiting room the faces on my family said it all. She was gone! At exactly 9:00!

Walking into the farmhouse later tore at my heart. It was so quiet, so empty. Their dog, Sarg, knew something was wrong and looked pitifully sad.

We lived two hours away from my dad and I tried to visit as often as I could. I felt like my grieving took longer than my siblings' as they lived closer and could be there almost every day. But each time I walked up the steps and into their kitchen she wasn't there. There were no homemade cookies to enjoy. It was like she should be coming out of her bedroom, or down the stairs, or I should hear her playing on her organ getting ready for another Sunday service. No, she was gone! And seeing how much my dad was hurting just broke my heart. It took many visits before I could walk into the farmhouse without crying. I always had to pray for peace, comfort and strength which the Lord faithfully gave me. (He would do it again).

So here I am with my memories. Mom is gone. The farm has changed; our lives have changed. But this is life. For most of us, we grow up in our safe and secure environments with our parents' love and protection. We believe our parents are invincible; we think everything will remain as perfect as we remember them during our childhood days. Sooner or later it all does become just "memories." This is life. "It is even a vapor that appears for a little time, and then vanishes away" James 4:14. The emptiness goes on these many years later, but I am treasuring those precious memories. Breaking through clouds of grief takes time, but my God has and continues to give me peace. Are these the clouds you find yourself in currently?

BE STILL AND.....

> We believe our parents are invincible; we think everything will remain as perfect as we remember them during our childhood days. Sooner or later it all does become just "memories." This is life.

READ THE WORD

"Who can find a virtuous woman? For her price is far above rubies. She openeth her mouth with wisdom; and in her tongue is the law of kindness. Her children arise up, and call her blessed; her husband also, and he praiseth her."
Proverbs 31:10, 26, 28

HIDE THE WORD

"For what is your life? It is even a vapor that appears for a little time and then vanishes away."
James 4:14

PRAY THE WORD

Dear Father, Thank you for the mother you gave to me and my siblings. To me, her days seemed to have been shortened, but her life was full and she was indeed a virtuous woman. I am thankful for the example she was to me. Amen.

KNOW THAT I AM GOD

Psalm 46:10

MEMORIES AND MEMORIALS

Memories! How important are they? I believe they are extremely important and that we should be building the most wonderful memories or memorials; not only for ourselves, but for our children. Remember what the Lord had Joshua do as they crossed the Jordan River into the Promised Land? They were to take 12 stones (one for each tribe of Israel) from the place where the priests stood in the middle of the riverbed and place them where they lodged. They were to be a memorial for their children. When they would ask, "What do these stones mean?" their fathers could tell them, *"For the LORD your God dried up the waters of Jordan from before you, until ye were passed over, as the LORD your God did to the Red sea, which he dried up from before us, until we were gone over: that all the people of the earth might know the hand of the LORD, that it is mighty: that ye might fear the LORD your God forever."* (Jos. 4:23,24).

We don't want to be slaves to our past; but as Christians, we can grow from our experiences (our memorials). I encourage you to remember what God has done for you in times past; remember how He has brought you this far, so in the future you can continue to trust Him to do the same. God brought me through a difficult time (**some very dark clouds**) in losing my mother. He would do it again!

We know that not all things ARE good, but God will use everything in our life FOR good. (Rom. 8:28, 29). God knows what your life's "finished tapestry" will look like. God will use all those threads of difficult, trying situations, to grow you, to mold you to become more like His Son. We just need to trust Him in the process. You can do this if you spend time reading, studying, getting to know our wonderful Lord personally. This is where my help and my strength come from – it's from nowhere or no one else. And He's the One who can and will help you **break through your clouds**.

Have you been taking your own walk down memory lane? I realize not everyone has pleasant memories of childhood days, of marriage, or of a lot of things or situations. You may even think "What good am I?" From the time we're born (and even before) God knew us and He is using every detail in our lives to help form us, mold us; to use all those different colored threads to produce a masterpiece (a tapestry of your life). Take time again and reread Psalm 139 and see how much God cares for you.

My tapestry is different from yours. We are all different. But none of us can see the finished work. All we see are the colored threads on the back; tangled, making no sense, some black in color, others bright and cheery. Much of how our tapestry turns out is up to us. But God is the weaver; and how we respond to life's trials and heartaches will determine what the finished side looks like.

> **The Tapestry**
> Corrie ten Boom
>
> My life is but a weaving
> between my Lord and me.
> I cannot choose the colors,
> He worketh steadily
> Oft times he weaveth sorrow,
> and I, in foolish pride,
> Forget he sees the upper
> And I the underside.
>
> Not 'til the loom is silent
> and the shuttles cease to fly
> Shall God unroll the canvas
> and explain the reason why
> The dark threads are as needful
> in the Weaver's skillful hands,
> as the threads of gold and silver
> In the pattern He has planned.

BE STILL AND.....

> Memories and memorials are extremely important. Sharing what God has brought you through will help establish and strengthen your faith and even build your children's faith.

READ THE WORD

"That all the people of the earth might know the hand of the LORD, that it is mighty: that ye might fear the LORD your God forever."
Jos. 4:24

HIDE THE WORD

"And we know that all things work together for good to them that love God, to them who are the called according to his purpose. For whom he did foreknow, he also did predestinate to be conformed to the image of his Son, that he might be the firstborn among many brethren."
Romans 8:28 29

PRAY THE WORD

Dear Father, I know that not all things that happen in my life are good; but I know you use them for my good. Please help me to trust You as You use those difficult and trying situations in my life to grow me and mold me to become more like your Son, the Lord Jesus Christ. Amen.

KNOW THAT I AM GOD

Psalm 46:10

TILL DEATH DO US PART

My husband, Autry, never had an actual heart attack, but over the years from 1993 to 2013 he had 2 open heart surgeries, and 18 stents put in his heart, along with several other tests and procedures. Every time he went into the hospital, my kids and I wondered, "Would he be okay? Is this it?" He was told in 1993 that he would probably have at least 10 more years to live. God granted him 20!

It was during the last year (2013) that I could tell he was having more and more difficulty; his breathing was more labored, and just walking from room to room was becoming more difficult. His diabetic issues didn't help any.

The week before Christmas in 2013 I was singing in our church musical in the morning service. I found him standing out in the foyer afterward. "I needed some air," he told me. "I couldn't stay in there any longer." We went home to where I had our dinner ready in the crock pot. It smelled so good. But before we could sit down, he said, "I really need to go to the hospital!" Dinner would wait.

The VA Hospital was about a 45-minute drive (which I probably drove in 30 minutes). It wasn't long after we arrived that they had him in a brightly lit ICU room, hooked up with all the wires and tubes. Once again, I couldn't believe what I was seeing and yet I really wasn't surprised. I hated leaving him that night, but I planted a kiss on his lips and said, "Good night. I'll see you in the morning."

I spent as much time with him as I could, but four days later when I arrived, his breathing was becoming more difficult as pneumonia had now set in. The doctor's plan and suggestion to me was to put him into an induced coma with the hope that his body would fight it off. After a few phone calls, the decision was made. "Yes, I agree and consent to this procedure."

The next several days, as he lay in that coma, were a blur with back-and-forth trips from the hospital to home and trying to prepare for all my kids and grandchildren who would be coming for Christmas.

Christmas morning was as normal as it could be with added tears; missing husband, dad, or grandpa. We had our dinner and then we all piled into cars to drive to the VA hospital in Buffalo. We had discussed and explained to the children what to expect when we entered his room, but to our amazement when we did enter his room, he was awake and alert; although still hooked up with wires and tubes and unable to speak as a result. A nurse brought in a small Christmas tree and placed it on a stand near his bed. We sang every Christmas Carol we could think of as my husband smiled that big 'ol smile even with a tube in his mouth. He had a large white pad on which he wrote little messages; basically, saying his "Good-by" to each of us. Two words he wrote to me were, "Almost home!" Although I knew the answer, I asked, "Home with me or home…?" and I looked up. He also looked up!

Leaving him that day tugged on all of our hearts, but we have called it our "Christmas Miracle," because he was alert and we got to enjoy his last Christmas with him.

That night the house was empty except for my daughter and me. At 2:00 in the morning the phone rang. I knocked it on the floor as I hurriedly tried to answer it in the dark and when I finally found it I heard the words I was dreading to hear; "Can you come? Your husband only has a few more hours to live!" Dressing quickly, making a few fast calls (including one to my pastor) and we were on our way; my daughter driving this time and totally ignoring any speed limits. We ran into the hospital, grabbed the elevator, and raced through hallways to the ICU. As soon as we saw Autry and saw him struggling to breathe as the nurses were working on him, we let him know we were there. But it was obvious what time it was. It was time to let him go; time for him to meet his Savior whom he loved and served as a pastor for 30 years. I held his hand as he lay there those final moments and my daughter softly sang in his ear, "Face to Face," until he took his final breath.

Approximately three months before his home-going, Autry had been teaching our Adult Bible Fellowship (senior saints' group) in our church. The topic was Revelation. He loved that study. One of the last lessons was on chapter 4 which describes the "throne room" in heaven. When he finished that day, he stood quietly for a moment and then said, "I can't wait to get there, can you?" I will always believe God was using that study to get my husband ready for the greatest day in his life – his death and his entrance into heaven where he would finally meet his Savior face to face. He had longed for that day for quite some time. He was home – no more pain! But how would I ever break through this cloud of grieving. Perhaps you have been there or are there now.

BE STILL AND.....

He was basically saying his "Good-by" to each of us. Two words he wrote to me were, "Almost home!" Although I knew the answer, I asked, "Home with me or home…?" and I looked up. He also looked up!

READ THE WORD

"In my Father's house are many mansions: if it were not so, I would have told you. I go to prepare a place for you.
John 14:2

HIDE THE WORD

"O death, where is thy sting? O grave, where is thy victory?
I Cor. 15:55

PRAY THE WORD

Dear Father, Thank you for the promise of heaven to those who have trusted You as their Savior. I know I will see my loved one again some day. Amen.

KNOW THAT I AM GOD

Psalm 46:10

TWO LIVES BECAME ONE

Only a few weeks before my husband was ushered into heaven; out of the blue one day he said to me, "We've had a good life together, haven't we?" "Yes, we have," I answered. And indeed, we had, once I realized he was the one I truly wanted to spend the rest of my life with.

In the late spring of 1960, the school we both attended held its annual sophomore/senior banquet. A serious softball game followed with Autry as the pitcher for the seniors and me for the sophomores. He asked to take me home afterward and since I just needed a ride home, I simply said, "Yes!" That was the start of a relationship that would eventually lead to marriage. But I always said, "It was my swing that caused him to notice me!"

Sad to say, I gave the poor guy a hard time for quite some time, resulting in him several months later to enlist in the Marine Corp. The evening his parents and I were taking him to the train station, the two of us were talking in their living room. He was standing in front of their couch with a large mirror on the wall behind it. As he gave me a hug, my eyes caught the two of us together in the mirror and my mind was saying, "You dummy! You really do love this guy, and now he's going to be gone!"

As we said good-bye at the station, he also said, "I left my class ring on my dresser. If you want it (which would mean we were going steady – I was his girl) take it when you get back to my parents' home." I didn't hesitate to do just that, and I never dated anyone else in my junior or senior year. We did most of our dating by mail (snail mail, at that) and as I learned more about him, I grew to love him more and more. It was during his first leave that we got engaged. Although I was young, I knew he was the one I wanted to marry, and I also knew it would be for keeps (just like my mom and dad). There would be no walking away if things got tough.

The same day as our wedding on June 30, 1962, found this young farm girl, hardly ever away from home and family, heading to Beaufort, SC where Autry was stationed in the Marine Corp, to make my new home. We wouldn't return to western NY until a year and a half later.

Things were tough, but we had each other. There was no phone to call home and share things with Mom or get some advice; car repairs always seemed to be an issue, finances were tight and on our first Christmas we couldn't even afford gifts for each other. We would throw our 50 cent pieces in a "doggy bank" on the fireplace mantle which came to our aid more than once or provided a "movie night out!" Most of our "dates" were going to the beach, or going fishing, anything that didn't cost money. I was alone much of the time when he was at the base and loneliness set in many days. How I missed not being able to talk to my mom. Those two and a half years really cemented our marriage. All we had was each other, and the more we did together the more love we had for each other. So, there were many different "clouds" in those early years that I had to break through.

I know every marriage has clouds to break through no matter how much you love each other. You are not your own, you belong to your mate. Selfish desires must be dealt with, sharing finances or learning how to live on one income can be challenging. Sharing time with in-laws and getting along with them is another challenge at times. What **clouds did you, or do you need to break through in your marriage?** God established marriage and with Him in the center of your lives, no cloud is impossible to break through.

BE STILL AND.....

> Although I was young, I knew he was the one I wanted to marry, and I also knew it would be for keeps (just like my mom and dad). There would be no walking away if things got tough.

READ THE WORD

"Entreat me not to leave you, or to turn back from following after you; For wherever you go, I will go; And wherever you lodge, I will lodge; your people shall be my people, And your God, my God. Where you die, I will die, and there will I be buried. The Lord do so to me, and more also, If anything but death parts you and me."
Ruth 1:16, 17

HIDE THE WORD

"Therefore shall a man leave his father and his mother, and shall cleave unto his wife: and they shall be one flesh."
Gen. 2:24

PRAY THE WORD

Dear Father, I thank you for the spouse you have given to me. Yes, we find ourselves in some clouds. Help me to never "walk away" but to lean on You for your help, strength, and direction. Give me wisdom and show me how I can be the wife you intended me to be. Amen.

KNOW THAT I AM GOD

Psalm 46:10

THE CLOUD OF SIN BROKEN

It was only a few months after we'd been married that the Cuban Missile Crisis began. In our four-apartment building, two of the men were in the navy, two in the Marine Corp. Two of them were sent to Key West where our military troops were on alert 24/7. Autry and the other marine were kept on the base outside of Beaufort, S.C. It would be days before he would come home and, of course, with no phone I didn't know what was going on. Before he left for the base, one of the things he said to me was, "If you see a bright light and hear a tremendous explosion, you'll know what that is!" He didn't have to say – atomic bomb! That first night he went to the base I will never forget. All night long you could hear the planes taking off from the base. Our bedroom window literally rattled all night long from the roaring of the planes.

Those were some of the hardest days of my life as I wasn't a Christian at that time (although my husband thought I was). I was scared and alone and couldn't call home. It was the first time I had ever thought, "I could die if we go to war!" I had no peace or hope.

Peace and hope wouldn't come until we moved back to western NY. A dear lady who worked in Autry's department invited us to attend her church, Westside Baptist Church in Rochester, NY. I was amazed that everyone brought a Bible, sermons were from scripture and there was a love and welcoming spirit I hadn't seen or felt before. Autry was drawn to rededicate his life to the Lord following one Sunday's message. I saw a change in his life and felt like something was missing in mine. One day not long after that, while I was home alone, the Holy Spirit helped me realize that I was a sinner in need of salvation. All I could do was fall prostrate on my face with tears flowing, confessing I was a sinner and accepting God's amazing gift of salvation through Jesus Christ my Lord.

I couldn't get enough of reading the word of God, and Galatians 2:20 soon became my life's verse. *"I am crucified with Christ, nevertheless I live; yet not I, but Christ lives in me; and the life that I now live in the flesh, I live by the faith of the son of God, who loved me, and gave himself for me."*

Even though we were young in the Lord, we became very involved in the church. I sang in the choir, taught in Vacation Bible School, was a leader in Pioneer Girls. Autry worked in the Boy's Brigade, and we both were leaders with the youth. God was growing us quickly in the things of the Lord.

I hope you have trusted the Lord as your Savior and that you have peace and hope in your soul. I hope that **the sin cloud** has been removed and you are on the way to heaven.

Breaking Through the Clouds

BE STILL AND.....

> One day not long after that, while I was home alone, the Holy Spirit helped me realize that I was a sinner in need of salvation. All I could do was fall prostrate on my face with tears flowing, confessing I was a sinner and accepting God's amazing gift of salvation through Jesus Christ my Lord.

READ THE WORD

"These things have I written to you that believe on the name of the Son of God, that you may know that you have eternal life."
I John 5:13

HIDE THE WORD

"I am crucified with Christ, nevertheless I live; yet not I, but Christ lives in me; and the life that I now live in the flesh, I live by the faith of the son of God, who loved me, and gave himself for me."
Gal. 2:20

PRAY THE WORD

Dear Father, I thank you for saving me and for living within me. I pray that you will help me to live by faith. Thank you for the assurance that I will be with you for eternity. Amen

KNOW THAT I AM GOD

Psalm 46:10

GOD'S CALL INTO MINISTRY

While we were building our dream home in Byron, NY, we became members of the Grace Baptist Church in Brockport. Once again, we became very involved in various ministries. Autry was a deacon, building committee chairman, was assistant pastor for a while, and worked in AWANA. I sang in the choir, became the church secretary, taught a Junior High Sunday School Class, did visitation with the pastor's wife, and held a Joy Club in my home, sometimes having as many as 30 children in my basement on Tuesdays after school. God continued to grow us in our faith and was teaching us many things which we would use in the future.

I knew for years that Autry's heart was to be in fulltime ministry as a pastor. But my heart was content to serve the Lord as a layperson in our local church and stay close to family. When it seemed to me that he was no longer bringing it up, I felt relieved. But then God began to do a work in my own heart. I felt that we really should be pursuing full-time ministry. Unfortunately, by this time, Autry had started a new sales job. Rather than tell him how I felt, I began to pray this prayer every day as he left for work: "Dear Lord, if you don't want Autry to continue in this job but want him to be in ministry, please don't let him get one sale!" Yes, the Lord answered that prayer – not one sale! It meant we would be on food stamps and max out two credit cards during those months. Several weeks later while at our supper table, he looked at me and said, "I'm going to go to Bible School whether you are ready or not." He didn't expect the simple answer I gave him, "I'm ready, too!" God was at work in each of our lives in different ways transforming us and calling us into ministry. Oh, God is so Good!

In June of 1979 Autry and I graduated from Elohim Bible Institute in Castile, NY. We had driven 40 miles one way, three times a week for 3 years; two evenings a week and on Saturday mornings for a total of 48,000 miles (as someone had figured out)! Autry maintained a different job and I was secretary at our home church. Each of us served in several different capacities in church. God was preparing us for what was ahead in the future, to the ministry where He would lead us.

We lived in our "dream home" for ten years. My father had given each of us kids two acres of land from his property. We were the first to build, hardly a quarter of a mile from the homestead. Our children had the privilege of being with their grandparents practically every day and enjoying some "life on the farm" as I had. Our swimming pool was an attraction that brought friends from church and parties and picnics with young and old alike. We all loved our home, and we opened it up for some very special fellowship times.

We knew the Lord was leading us into home missions and we sold our home, not knowing exactly where that field was going to be and where we would live in the meantime. For months before this, every time I drove into the driveway, I would sit crying and saying to the Lord, "How can I leave this home and Mom and Dad up the road?" My husband, on the other hand, was dealing with leaving the security of a very good job. And what about our children? Leaving their home of ten years, leaving friends and school (one was a sophomore, one a freshman and one a fifth grader) would not be easy. But, oh, how the Lord undertook for all of us. When we signed those closing papers, I never shed a tear and never regretted making that decision to follow the Lord wherever He would lead us. My husband felt the same.

The Lord graciously led us to temporary housing at a sister church that had a home they opened to missionaries on pre-field ministry. As we settled in, I ventured into one closet off the living room and squealed with excitement as I found a small plaque on the wall which read: "God is too good to be unkind, and too wise to make a mistake." Were we in the right place? We had chosen ***I Thess. 5:17*** as our ministry verse before all of this: ***"Faithful is He that*** *calleth you, who also will do it."* We also would often come back to ***Proverbs 3:5, 6 "Trust in the Lord with all your heart. Lean not unto your own understanding. In all your ways acknowledge Him and He will direct your path."***

I've often thought about Abraham and how God had called him and his family to leave their home and country and go to a place where God would show him. Abraham had no idea where that was. I can only imagine how Sarah must have felt. But they obeyed and God led them all the way. No, it's not always easy to follow the Lord when He wants you to make a change; to move, or to serve Him in some different area. We might want to run in the opposite direction, but oh, the blessings we would miss if we did that. There may be nothing but **dark clouds** hiding the path ahead of you. Remember, we cannot see the future, but God can. We just need to be willing to have a submissive spirit and follow and trust His leadership.

BE STILL AND.....

> Several weeks later while at our supper table, he looked at me and said, "I'm going to go to Bible School whether you are ready or not." He didn't expect the simple answer I gave him, "I'm ready, too!"

READ THE WORD

"Trust in the Lord with all your heart. Lean not unto your own understanding. In all your ways acknowledge Him and He will direct your path."
Proverbs 3:5, 6

HIDE THE WORD

"Faithful is He that calleth you, who also will do it."
I Thess. 5:17

PRAY THE WORD

Dear Father, I see nothing but dark clouds hiding the path ahead of us. I don't know what you want us to do. But I know you are faithul and I trust your leading in our lives. I know you won't let us make a mistake. Amen

KNOW THAT I AM GOD

Psalm 46:10

MINISTRY YEARS

(Part 1)

PENSACOLA, FLORIDA

After several months of deputation (which they called it back then), trying to raise support to go to the field we believed God was calling us to, the day came to pack up and move once again, but this time to our first ministry in Pensacola, FL. There was a small group of believers that had called us to help them start a new church after we had made a trip down to meet with them and to see how the Lord would lead. During that week, they called us to come, and we immediately set out to find a home to purchase. In only a few days, we found that home and signed all the papers before heading back up north. The "good-byes" were bittersweet as we left the state of New York. But when we arrived at our new home there was a large banner across the front of our home which read, "Welcome Burlings!" We had no idea what all was ahead.

We knew God had called us and led us to Florida, but we ended up calling our time there our "Wilderness Experience." The Lord taught us so many things and we claimed our ministry verse (***"Faithful is He that calleth you, who also will do it." I Thess. 5:17***) so often, and we found Him to be truly faithful and enabled us to complete many projects for this new work. As home missionaries we never had our full support, so finances were always a struggle for us from day one. However, God always provided our needs. He never failed.

Our services were held in a YMCA for a while, then in a school, and even in our home until we were able to purchase a burned-out building. We had missionary builders come, tear down the burned-out building, and build a lovely church facility called Gulf Coast Baptist Church. From the burned-out building, we brought all the good boards into our backyard where for hours another lady and I would hammer out the nails so the boards could be reused in the new building. I also spent many other hours chipping off old mortar from cement blocks that could also be reused. It was hot and tiring work. But we also had fun with the missionary builders. Ed (one of the builders) called me his "slave" as he would ask me to bring various things to him so he could keep working. I sent cookies one day with Autry to the worksite with a note saying: "For slave-driver from Slave!" He loved that.

One dear family from back in western New York did supply the funds for our children to attend a Christian school; but we had a rude awakening when we took them to the school to register. Their dress code was very strict and as they looked our children over, they said, "That style of pants isn't acceptable; the dress length on your daughter needs to be 2" below the knees. Oh, and the boy's hair needs to be shorter." My husband and I just looked at each other, knowing the kids were hurting and probably fuming inside. None of us spoke as we rode home. Two hours later, after much time praying for our children, it was time! "Boys," Autry said, "It's time to go to the barber shop and then we need to do some shopping." The only thing we ever heard from the kids came from our oldest son who said, "If you had asked me two hours ago, I would not have done it!" They did adjust to their new school but also found out quickly that more was expected from them because they were "a pastor's kid!"

To help with the bills, I worked some "less than glamorous" jobs; even assisting my kids with delivering newspapers early mornings and late afternoons. I got really good driving down the streets in my car with my window down and flinging the bagged papers onto the lawns! It was almost fun, but very hot.

My hardest job physically was being a substitute mail carrier. Bundling the mail into stacks and having to lift them from the backseat of my car to the front put a terrible strain on my shoulder. My route was the longest one in that office. Because it was so hot, I would bring a large thermos canister of water and a wash cloth and stop at one of my more secluded spots and just wipe myself down. Often my husband would track me down and bring me a "Big Gulp" from 711.

I was told by my instructor not to drive down one of the roads if it was raining because the road wasn't paved – it was all red clay. It had only started to sprinkle one day, and I thought there was time to drive the 2 mile stretch to the end and turn around and come back to the highway. It wasn't long, however, when the sprinkles turned into a downpour and quickly turned the road into a soupy mess. My car swerved back and forth and was drawn backwards into a ditch. There I was – thunder and lightning, pouring rain and tears flowing almost as hard down my face. "Lord, I need your help," was all I could say. Rain, hail, sleet, or snow – the mail must go through; and each of us drivers was expected to make it back on our own one way or another. The Lord reminded me – I was a New Yorker! I knew how to get out of a snowbank so I applied the same principles. I rocked my car back and forth (drive to reverse) several times and then I hit the gas pedal. I must have shot the mud 30 feet in the air, but I got out. The car needed a wash after that, but the mail got through!

I had forgotten to pack my lunch another day and brought no money with me, so I couldn't even stop at a drive-thru. However, as I opened the lid on one of the mailboxes I was blessed with cookies and candy "for the mailman." It was kind of a crazy lunch, but I so appreciated it. I called it "my manna in the mailbox!" God knew I would need this on this day and had a lady baking them for me probably the day before with no idea what a blessing she would be.

Our oldest son, Preston, graduated while we were in Pensacola. He was accepted at Baptist Bible College in Clarks Summit, PA. We packed him up, made a trip to western New York for him to see his grandparents before entering a new phase of his life. The college held a special welcoming ceremony for the freshman class and their parents. As they talked to the students and to the parents, the tears started to flow more and more. At one point I had to walk out just to contain myself. My "first-born" wouldn't be coming back home with us to Pensacola, FL. That was so far away. Saying our good-byes just tugged at my heart strings and the ride home was quiet except for my sobbing. Anyone who has grown up on a farm will understand when I say, "I felt like a mother cow which just had her calf taken away from her!" That is one of the most pitiful sounds ever on a farm.

There were several things that I had to do while in Pensacola that I never thought I could do. When I thought I couldn't go on I was reminded of **Phil. 4:13, *"I can do all things through Christ which strengthens me."*** There was a lot of physical work in this first ministry as well as the normal things that needed to be done in being a pastor and pastor's wife in a church. But we were able to minister with this group of people long enough to see them through the purchasing process of the land and of a burned-out building and continued to minister for several months after the completion of a lovely new facility. We stayed long enough for them to call a different pastor, who would continue to lead them as we moved on to our next place of ministry.

We were always thankful for the way God had prepared us for fulltime ministry with our involvement in our previous churches as lay people. But now it was different and there were many dark clouds that faced us: setbacks and discouragements, long days of actual physical labor even for me, the Florida heat, trying to grow the church and work on the physical building, and feeling the hand of Satan trying to disrupt. We were often faced with *D.D.D.S* (the Devil's Devious Doubting Syndrome"). Remember that earlier in my book? Things like: "nothing seems to be happening, we must be doing something wrong, maybe we shouldn't be here, how can we keep going, maybe we really aren't qualified for this work. If you are in ministry in any way (doesn't have to be fulltime), you may feel the same things. Satan loves to play games with your mind. Don't listen to him. In order to **break through those clouds** of doubt and discouragement you need to stay focused on God's word and His promises. God says in ***Joshua 1:5, 6 "I will be with thee: I will not fail thee, or forsake thee. Be strong and of a good courage."*** His word will not return void. Remember, we are not all the same. We all have different talents and abilities. He will use you when you surrender to Him. He will enable you to do what He wants you to do.

BE STILL AND.....

> We knew God had called us and led us to Florida, but we ended up calling our time there our "Wilderness Experience."

READ THE WORD

*"I will be with thee: I will not fail thee or forsake thee.
Be strong and of a good courage."*
Joshua 1:5, 6

HIDE THE WORD

"But my God shall supply all your needs according to His riches in glory."
Phil. 4:13

PRAY THE WORD

Dear Father, Thank you for your promise and your encouragement that You will be with me and You won't forsake me (even when I feel like a failure). I know you will supply my needs physically, but I also pray You will strengthen me spiritually so You can use me to serve You better. Amen

KNOW THAT I AM GOD

Psalm 46:10

MINISTRY YEARS

(Part 2)

I loved being a pastor's wife. I felt the Lord was using my talents and abilities in each of our churches. I was the church secretary in each church, played the piano or organ and directed the choir, was a Sunday school teacher, youth director and taught a ladies Bible study. Several times I wrote plays for Christmas, skits for Vacation Bible School, and articles for newsletters. The one thing I lacked was someone I could talk to on a personal level other than my pastor husband. It just seemed that a pastor's wife is a "different breed!" I think people see us or put us on a pedestal and think we are above them. How untrue. We're no different from anyone else.

That's what Connie realized when we were at our next place of ministry – Kennedy, New York.

KENNEDY, N.Y.

Connie became my close friend; brought me out of my shell and made me realize I could let my hair down and have fun. She made me laugh, especially with her holding me up in the air on a teeter/totter in a park, banging pots and pans together at midnight outside her home on New Year's Eve or enjoying a breakfast of waffles with warm peaches and a scoop of vanilla ice cream on top. But we also shared spiritual things. We'd get together at my kitchen table and often talk about things going on at the church. We guarded ourselves, realizing we didn't want our time together to turn into a complaining session or a gossip session. So, we had our prayer time and challenged each other with memorizing scripture and listening to one another recite our verses. Our biggest challenge was memorizing Romans, chapter 8. After all these years later, I still can quote it without too many mistakes.

Connie and I were invited to a shower given by a lady in town-- not one from our church. I asked Connie, "What should I wear?" She said, "You'd have the greatest impact on those ladies from the town if you'd wear jeans." For the most part I had only worn a dress or skirt and top since being in the ministry. "Jeans?" I wrestled with the idea and prayed and opened my Bible. Turning to several sections, I found something Paul wrote in I Corinthians 9:19, 20, 22, 23: "... Yet have I made myself servant unto all, that I might gain the more. And unto the Jews I became as a Jew, that I might gain the Jews…To the weak became I as weak, that I might gain the weak: I am made all things to all men, that I might by all means save some. And this I do for the gospel's sake…" Jeans it would be! But I didn't own any. Going into my son's bedroom I found a pair of his jeans that fit. As I walked into that home for the shower, Connie was already sitting on the couch. She looked at me with the biggest smile on her face and without saying a word her eyes were giving a big thumbs up!

The first workday at church after this event I wore jeans. (I think I bought some). I was at the top of the wide staircase going into the sanctuary and a lady at the bottom called out, "Marlene, you look so nice in jeans!" The change began. **God had helped me to break through my clouds of fear and acceptance** and I felt free for the first time to be me!

There would be other friends through the years. I just knew there would be things I couldn't share regarding ministry things. That would transpire between me and my husband – my best friend!

This ministry was a rescue work. They had been ready to close their doors when they called us. We ministered there for nine and a half years. There was a lot of physical work in this ministry also. It was an older building and needed lots of repair inside and out. Of course, Autry had his regular duties as Pastor, but he also led in all of the physical things that needed to be done. I was the church secretary, the church pianist, was able to start a choir, taught a teen Sunday school class, worked with the youth, taught a ladies' Bible study and was involved in our lady's missionary group. I also loved to visit the older ladies of our church, mostly who were widows. I think this had a greater impact on me than I realized as in later years this would be a major ministry in my life.

At the start of this work, I always felt so blessed by the Lord and thankful that we didn't have all the trials and heartaches that so many others had. However, I also knew God does allow hardships in our lives to make us more like Him. I remember specifically looking out my kitchen window one day and thinking to myself, "If God loves us (which I know He does) then I can expect there are going to be some difficult things we are going to experience. I believe they will be coming." And come they did.

There were many **dark clouds** that had hovered over the people and yes, even the small town for several years. So, as the old church building needed repairs, other things also needed *repairs*: mending of old hurts and division was a struggle, establishing a good testimony in the town took time and even dealing with a discipline problem was probably the hardest. And as the church itself was going through a very difficult time, we were also struggling with some personal situations. Part of that was losing my mother. (That story is in a previous section). Our last child went off to college and we had to adjust to the empty nest syndrome, our son and daughter-in-law had their first baby (our second grandchild) – a little boy, born with Down Syndrome. (The article I wrote about his birth is in the next section).

At times it would have been so easy to just walk away from it all as we often thought, "There's no use, we can't do this, we are tired." And, no, we couldn't do it. It wasn't up to us. It was the Lord's work: His timing, His moving in the lives of individuals. We just had to be faithful and trust and obey and let God use us in whatever way He wanted. That was the only way to **break through those clouds.** Yes, there were many hardships but there were also many more blessings as we left a stable church in the hands of another preacher.

Breaking Through the Clouds

BE STILL AND.....

> As the church itself was going through a very difficult time, we were also struggling with some personal situations. It would have been so easy to just walk away from it all.

READ THE WORD

"...Yet have I made myself servant unto all, that I might gain the more. And unto the Jews I became as a Jew, that I might gain the Jews... To the weak became I as weak, that I might gain the weak: I am made all things to all men, that I might by all means save some. And this I do for the gospel's sake..."
I Corinthians 9:19, 20, 22, 23

HIDE THE WORD

"So then neither is he that planteth anything, neither he that watereth; but God that giveth the increase."
I Cor. 3:7

PRAY THE WORD

Dear Father, Ministry isn't easy. Serving You can be hard and discouraging at times. But this isn't our work, it's Yours. Help us to be faithful and to simply trust and obey knowing that in your time there will be increase. Amen

KNOW THAT I AM GOD

Psalm 46:10

MINISTRY YEARS

(Part 2 continued)

While dealing with several situations at Kennedy, the phone rang one day with news of the birth of our first grandson. This is the article I wrote several months later.

HAPPINESS IS....SHANE BRYAN

Shane Bryan came into our lives on July 6, 1989. The phone rang exceptionally early that morning, causing our hearts to beat a little faster. Hearing our son's tired, but excited voice, we knew right away we were grandparents once again. Yes, Shane Bryan, all of 7 pounds, 5 ounces, and 20-1/2 inches long would be a delightful new addition to our family.

I couldn't wait to share my joy, and as soon as a reasonable hour was shown on the clock, my fingers excitedly dialed every number I could think of. What a joy to share the good news of the birth of a little boy.

Later in the day, while still pondering what he would look like and what he would grow up to be, the phone rang again. It was Lyle, his voice broken this time as he faintly informed us, "The doctors suspect Shane is a Down Syndrome baby!"

The news was overwhelming and I'm not even sure what transpired in the remainder of the conversation. But I do remember us saying, "We're coming down." Not only my husband and I, but our other son and his wife and Lyle's in-laws responded quickly and rushed to their side to be whatever comfort and support we could.

The five-hour trip seemed to drag on endlessly--my thoughts and emotions were a mixture of questions, of fears, of concern, and yet of peace. God was in total control... I had no doubt about this.

Walking into the hospital room I felt a lump in my throat. Hugs were exchanged and perhaps they said more than any spoken word. Soon, Shane was brought into the room and each of us took our turn holding this new little bundle. Immediately his little eyes told the story. He was a Down Syndrome baby. I squeezed my new little grandson and the tears flowed, not out of pity, anger or disappointment, but out of love. God had chosen a special family to give Shane to. He would be loved.

There are those in the world who, had they known they were carrying a Downs child, would have terminated that little life. What a tragedy! God doesn't make any mistakes and He knew Shane would be a special child from the moment of conception, when somehow an extra chromosome was added to his cells. He knew everything about this little life as Shane was developing in his mother's womb. What a loss, had we not had the privilege of this new baby boy!

Over the next two years, with much work and patience on the part of Shane's mother, Sharie, it was exciting to watch Shane progress. Simple feats like stacking eight or ten blocks or reassembling a four-piece puzzle have been accomplishments for which to rejoice. He is walking now, and his vocabulary is growing and I'm sure I've heard him say, "Grandma!" He is generous with hugs, loves to give away kisses, and has a smile that will make you melt.

As of August 22, 1991, Shane has a new baby sister. Adjustments may be a little difficult for him, but I'm sure there is enough love in his little heart for one more. They will be good for each other, and I know one day his little sister, Marlene Jo, will be able to say right along with the rest of us, "Happiness is.... Shane Bryan!"

If you have a "special child" you are blessed. God has given him/her to you. Yes, there may be some **dark and heavy clouds** ahead of you, but God will give you wisdom and strength. He will help you **break through those clouds** when you think there is no possible way through.

BE STILL AND…..

> God doesn't make any mistakes. He knew Shane would be a special child from the moment of conception. What a loss, had we not had the privilege of this new baby boy!

READ THE WORD

"For thou hast possessed my reins: thou hast covered me in my mother's womb. I will praise thee; for I am fearfully and wonderfully made: marvelous are thy works; and that my soul knoweth right well."
Psalm 139:13,14

HIDE THE WORD

"Children are an heritage of the LORD: and the fruit of the womb is his reward."
Psalm 127:3

PRAY THE WORD

Dear Father, I thank you for each of the children you have given to me. You formed each one of them while they were in my womb. You knew exactly what they would look like. You know what lie ahead for each of them. Give me wisdom as I nurture them in the things of You. Keep them Father, close to your heart. Amen

KNOW THAT I AM GOD

Psalm 46:10

MINISTRY YEARS

(Part 3)

A DISAPPOINTING CALL

It was never easy leaving one church and going to another. I hated good-byes. There were times when we felt the Lord was leading us to a particular church, but then it was made clear to us that the Lord had other plans in mind for us.

One such church was in Pennsylvania. We had met with the deacons in that church along with their "search committee," and were called to come and candidate. They felt we were a "perfect fit" for them. Services went great, the reception dinner was wonderful, and we were already falling in love with the people. Following the evening service was their business meeting and time to vote. However, there had been several people who hadn't been attending any of the services for some time because of disagreements but had together decided to come for this important vote.

We were anxiously waiting in our motel room for the results. The knock came on the door and six deacons walked in, literally with tears in their eyes. The vote result was obvious. More tears and hugs and good-byes, but also knowing God is sovereign – He is in control – He won't fail us; and He never did. He would lead us to where He wanted us next. Studying the Word of God and praying diligently kept our minds focused on the right direction as we waited for God to open another door of ministry

STRODES MILLS, PA

It was interesting how the Lord led us to our next ministry. One of our families in Kennedy moved out of state and had heard of another church in Pennsylvania that was looking for a pastor who could help them with a particular need they had. She contacted us and explained the situation. After praying about it, we felt the Lord was once again directing our steps into another area of ministry for which He had been equipping us. We just didn't know how difficult it would end up being.

They had wanted to pull out of a convention they were associated with as it was doctrinally headed in the wrong direction. Their desire was to become an independent church. This was something that Autry would spend over a year praying about and preparing the people for such a decision. It would be very important for the church to do so. When the time came, the vote was positive and, yes, good for the church.

It was during our 9 years of ministry here that Autry had his first issue with his heart. We had been walking 4 miles a day in an hour's time and enjoying that time together. One morning we had gone less than a mile and he had to stop as he was experiencing pain in his chest. He sat on the side of the road while I ran home for the car. Resting awhile, the pain subsided, and he dismissed it as acid reflux or heart burn. But this was a Wednesday and Wednesday night meant Prayer Meeting. He walked to church as it was only a brief walk away, but once inside, he was not able to climb the steep stairs to the sanctuary. Sharp pains brought him to a standstill. It was the next day the doctor had him come in right away and then to the hospital where the news of heart surgery hit like a ton of bricks. (Details of this are in my opening chapter)

We really thought we were eventually going to retire from this church in Strodes Mills and settle in this area. We loved the church, the people, the beautiful countryside and things seemed to be going very well. We also felt the Lord had led us to a particular plot of land and we began building what we thought was going to be our retirement home which would include room for Autry's parents to come and live with us. I guess I'll never really understand what happened, but things began to change; people began to change and before we knew it, after nine years of ministry in this church, our time was concluded.

A statement that has always been an encouragement to me is: God doesn't call us to be successful; He wants us to be faithful. So, I reminded myself often when we were going through **dark clouds of disappointments and discouragements, setbacks, and even attacks of various kinds**, to keep focused on the Lord and keep doing, no matter what, the work of the ministry He has called us to do.

<u>*A PAUSE IN MINISTRY*</u>

We had to sell our unfinished home, put all of our furnishings and belongings into storage and go back to Western New York. We lived with my dad for a year and a half. God really used this time in our lives. I believe He knew we just needed "a respite;" physically and emotionally. We had some wonderful times with my dad and the rest of our family. My sister, who is 12 years younger than I, became my best friend as we got to spend many wonderful times together. We realized just how much we were alike and would even purchase identical things when we were apart. The Lord also undertook financially once again as my husband worked for a local farmer for a while and I was able to do some substitute teaching in several area schools. I even played the piano for a musical at the school I graduated from. Autry also became an assistant pastor temporarily before God opened the door for our next ministry.

Being out of the ministry for that time was so difficult, even though we felt it was beneficial for us. The waiting was hard, but we continued to pray that God, in His time, would again show us where He wanted us to serve. We kept remembering our ministry verse, "Faithful is He that calls you who will also do it." And He did just that. Oh, what a wonderful God!

BE STILL AND.....

> After praying about it, we felt the Lord was once again directing our steps into another area of ministry for which He had been equipping us. We just didn't know how difficult it would end up being.

READ THE WORD

"Be strong in the grace that is in Christ Jesus.... Thou therefore endure hardness, as a good soldier of Jesus Christ."
II Tim. 2:1, 3

HIDE THE WORD

"Many are the afflictions of the righteous: but the Lord delivers him out of them all."
Psalm 34:19

PRAY THE WORD

Dear Father, I continue to ask You to give us the strength we need in these challenging and discouraging times. Help us to endure as a soldier of Jesus Christ. I am trusting You to deliver us and give us victory. Amen

KNOW THAT I AM GOD

Psalm 46:10

MINISTRY YEARS

(Part 4)

NIAGARA FALLS, N.Y.

It was almost like coming back home (practically full circle) – Niagara Falls, NY. Wow! And we were only an hour from our parents and my siblings. Autry and I were together practically every day as I also worked in the church office as the secretary. We did a lot of visiting together. I was also the organist and choir director which I loved doing, as well as teaching Bible classes and working in AWANA. Our schedule was full.

We had our own home in Niagara Falls. We had lots of entertainment – meals and picnics. One of our favorite ministries there was with our seniors group, The OWLS (older, wiser, loving saints). We met once a month and went on all kinds of outings from boat rides to overnight trips to Sight & Sound in Lancaster, PA. Autry and I loved putting on skits; our favorites – dressing as one person with him behind me and his arms acting like mine; only he couldn't see what he was doing. There was "Gertie Gordon" (me **trying** to stir up a cake - what a mess!) and of course there was "Shorty Longfellow," doing exercises among other things – even a split! We were the entertainment for several of our dinners--not your typical pastor and pastor's wife! My husband was a fun-loving person and loved his people, as I did. We may not have had many "best friends" but we had a lot of good friends and we certainly had a lot of fond memories.

It was here in Niagara Falls that my husband's health began to go down quickly during our last year there. Autry began to realize that it was going to be time to retire. This was probably the hardest decision he ever had to make as he loved being in the ministry. He loved the Lord, He loved his people, and had hoped to keep preaching for many more years. But his body was saying otherwise.

Toward the end of the year, I put together a combination of a Thanksgiving and Christmas Cantata (pulling music from previous performances) for our choir. I guess you could say it was our finale! But, oh, how we both hated saying those final good-byes.

Each ministry held its own difficulties and problems as well as personal things we had to face. We may lay out our own plans and hopes of things we want to accomplish, but God often has other things in mind. Our disappointments are often His appointments! But remember, Jesus will never fail us. He is always faithful and directing our lives even through those **dark clouds of disappointment.**

BE STILL AND.....

> We may lay out our own plans and hopes of things we want to accomplish, but God often has other things in mind. Our disappointments are often His appointments! But remember: Jesus will never fail us. He is always faithful.

READ THE WORD

"Trust in the Lord with all your heart and lean not unto your own understanding. In all your ways acknowledge Him and He will direct your path.
Prov. 3:5, 6

HIDE THE WORD

"Faithful is He that calls you, who also will do it."
I Thess. 5:24

PRAY THE WORD

Dear Father, Right now I don't understand why things are going the way they are. But I am going to trust you with all my heart and ask that You will direct my path. You are a faithful God, and I know you will accomplish what you want for my life. Thank you. Amen

KNOW THAT I AM GOD

Psalm 46:10

CARE-GIVING FOR MY DAD

(Part One)

This section of my book is very precious to me. It was a very difficult time in our lives but a time that I would not have traded for anything in the world. It all took place while we were in our ministry in Niagara Falls, NY. I have chosen to pull dates and happenings right from the diary/journal I wrote during this time. For anyone who has been or is presently a caregiver, you will probably relive many of the things I will share or at least understand completely. For others, perhaps it will help you to understand what a caregiver goes through and how difficult it can be; and help you to know how to pray for them and reach out to them in whatever way you can. For me, there were **all kinds of clouds** that God helped me to break through: doubting my ability, making right decisions, knowing when to "let go."

April 2004

Dad was having extreme difficulty breathing. He was never one to go to a doctor or a hospital and resisted it "tooth and nail." I went out to see him on Saturday, the week before Easter. I convinced him to let me take him to the emergency room After several hours there he absolutely refused to be admitted, even though the doctor and I pleaded with him and let him know the seriousness of his heart condition. We walked out of the hospital – Dad with what I thought was a death sentence, and me with a knife in my own heart. There was nothing I could do.

Sunday morning came and Dad's condition worsened. He broke down the barriers he had built, and called my brother, Mel, and was soon on the way to the hospital again – this time being admitted. The prognosis was not good – he had been experiencing "silent" heart attacks. The next several days were traumatic for Dad. He could never stay in one place for any length of time and a long hospital stay was not a part of his agenda. We kids had to intervene more than once to get him to agree to stay as long as he did. This was a feat in itself.

Dad was released to go home with a visiting nurse to come to see him and meals on wheels were scheduled. Neither one lasted very long.

Dad continued to do his own cooking, mowing the lawn, putting in a little garden in the summer, and driving his car. But we could see big changes in his health; a gradual deterioration and weakness setting in.

December 15

By this time Dad couldn't make it out to the mailbox anymore, he couldn't feed his kitties, and he wasn't up to going out for his weekly Friday night fish fry. He became extremely lonesome with no outside contact and lost yet another lady friend. It seems he was one of the few his age left. I tried to get out as often as I could. The last time I took him for a fish fry it was extremely hard for him to walk into the restaurant. Previous to this visit, I had taken Dad for a ride around the countryside to see some of his childhood stomping grounds. He really enjoyed that. But then came......

December 20

Dad was scheduled to go to the doctor, but when my brother, Mel, and sister, Lyn, arrived Dad couldn't get out of his chair. He was extremely weak. He was taken by ambulance to United Memorial in Batavia, NY. After a lengthy examination in the ER, he was admitted. Once again, the prognosis was not good but it would be several days before we knew just how bad it was. Dad never complained about pain and even though he wanted to go back home to the farm he finally realized in his weakened condition he wouldn't be able to. Not only did he have heart problems, but Leukemia was now diagnosed. This was the culprit causing much of his weakness. Blood transfusions were ordered, and they seemed to perk him up somewhat.

We had several family conferences discussing what should be done, not only with Dad, but also the farm. Autry and I decided we would bring Dad home to live with us. We arranged a meeting in a conference room with Dad and all of us kids. Autry was our spokesperson, and I was so proud of him. He helped Dad understand what was transpiring in his life and that he simply couldn't return home, and we wanted him to come and live with us. It was a heart wrenching day for all of us.

Dad spent a month in United Memorial and then, as Medicare wouldn't cover any more days in the hospital, he was sent to the Waters (a nursing home facility) in East Aurora. How sad nothing was available in Genesee County. The Waters was a wonderful facility, but almost an hour's drive for all of us. He was in their rehab center and did well, but time was limited to 21 days, because of Medicare.

February 2005

Autry and I are about to begin a journey down a new path in life. I anticipate it's going to have a lot of rocks and bumps along the way. I can't see around the bends and corners, but my Lord and Savior Jesus Christ can. If I were to make this journey alone, I'd be filled with fear and anxiety; but the wonderful thing about it is my Savior walks with me. He knew this path was coming for me. He knows what lies ahead. I know there will be times when He'll more than "walk" with me— He'll carry me because I know I won't have the strength in myself to keep going. I have no idea how long this journey is going to take. That's not important; but what is important to me is that Jesus Christ will be magnified in my life – that others will see Him in me, and that I will be a blessing to my dad.

February 2, 2005

We met with the discharge planners. They were extremely helpful and said they would set up all the necessary things for Dad – visiting nurse, oxygen, lifeline. My brothers came and helped to set up his room in our home, downstairs. The room looks really nice and I picked up the farm picture and some other things for his room to help make him feel "at home." We purchased several other things we felt he would need.

February 10

This started the new journey of our lives down a path we had not experienced before. We picked up Dad about 11:30. My heart is still breaking for him because I know he would rather be going back home to the farm. I wish he was able to but he can't and I will do all I can to make him comfortable. He didn't want any lunch, but asked for some ice cream and was pleased when I brought him a good-sized bowl of chocolate. Autry took care of getting all of Dad's prescriptions – all 10 of them and organized all of them for me.

February 11

I began our morning rituals – it was "bath time!" I had for weeks been trying to figure out how to go about this. It worked out well. I hold up a sheet and ask him to "help me out" when it comes to the "down below area!" It certainly was an experience for both of us. I know it's about killing him for me to have to do some of the things I'm doing.

The visiting nurse came and was here for a couple of hours. She was very helpful. She asked Dad about an aide coming to help with a bath. He looked at her and then at me and said, "She does a good job!"

February 13

It just seems to me that Dad has given up. He looks so pitiful lying there. This whole thing is as emotionally draining as it is physically. It's just so hard to see him like this.

February 14

I have such a jewel for a husband. He loves my dad, too. Autry spent a long-time shaving dad. It must have been several weeks since the last time which was probably when Autry did it at rehab. His beard was tough, but Autry got it after using first hair clippers, then an electric shaver and finally the razor! Dad looked good. He had some cider, which always puts a smile on his face, and I read some cards he had received and gave him his favorite treat – ice cream.

I have reread the verses at the bottom of this journal many times. They are all a blessing to me. My favorite is Psalm 46:1, "God is our refuge and strength, a very present help in trouble." I know God is my strength and He is showering me with his grace during this time. There will be many purposes fulfilled in the coming days – some for myself and some for others.

It is 9:00 pm – I just went in to Dad and got him set for the night. I bought him a little tiger with red heart chocolates for Valentine's Day. He wanted one of the candies. I told him we've got to come up with a name for his tiger. He didn't hesitate one moment and said, "Marlene." So "Marlene" is sitting next to him on his stand.

February 15

Life just about drained out of me when I heard a loud thud and a weak holler. There was Dad lying on the floor. He had slipped and gone down on his right side and elbow. When I realized nothing was broken and he was okay, I tried to get him up. His feet wouldn't stay under him. I did more lifting than I should have as tonight the results are "talking to me!" But I was finally able to get him back on the bed.

Psalm 18:2 was perfect for me to see today. "The Lord is my rock, and my fortress, and my deliverer; my God, my strength, in whom I will trust."

So many times, when I am at my limit's end, I turn to the Book of Psalms. They are so comforting, and this is where my strength and help comes from.

February 17

Dad asked for just ice cream and coffee for supper. I did give him that, but I also gave him a "Milk Shake" made with Carnation Instant

Breakfast and a little vanilla ice cream in it. Boy, was that a hit. He took one sip and went "Mmmmm!" No problem getting him to drink all that! Psalm 71:14 "But I will hope continually and will yet praise thee more and more." Yes, Lord, I praise you more and more. I told Autry this morning "I wouldn't want to have missed out on any of this. I wouldn't have changed a thing. The Lord is blessing me in so many ways."

February 21

My daughter, Christine, and family came to visit as well as my sister, Lyn. Dad sat in his wheelchair for about three hours with all of us. It was great but he did get tired. The visit was so good for him. I am convinced more and more that having people around him is what he needs. It was hard for the grandchildren to say "Good-bye." It was hard for all of us. There are just a lot of emotions flying around here lately.

February 25

We got some news that we've known would be coming but hearing it for the first time was heart wrenching. Dad needs another blood transfusion. His white blood cell count went from 19,000 to 27,000 in a matter of days, so his body is not fighting it. The prognosis is not good. His primary care doctor is going to get the wheels in motion for hospice (it's hard to even write the word). I don't know how soon this will transpire but I expect it won't be long. My prayer now (and has been) that Dad won't suffer, and the Lord would just take him quickly. He is so unhappy away from the farm.

BE STILL AND.....

> I have no idea how long this journey is going to take. That's not important; but what is important to me is that Jesus Christ will be magnified in my life – that others will see Him in me, and that I will be a blessing to my dad.

READ THE WORD

"The Lord is my rock, and my fortress, and my deliverer; my God, my strength, in whom I will trust."
Psalm 18:2

HIDE THE WORD

"Be of good courage, and He shall strengthen your heart, all you that hope in the Lord."
Psalm 31:24

PRAY THE WORD

Dear Father, I need your strength to keep going. My burdens are too heavy for me to bear alone. I will trust in you because you are my rock, my fortress, and my deliverer. My hope is in no one else but You. Give me courage to press on. Make me strong. Amen

KNOW THAT I AM GOD

Psalm 46:10

CARE-GIVING FOR MY DAD

(Part Two)

February 26

The Lord gave us a beautiful day to take Dad out to see the farm. We took the back way where Dad could see some familiar territory – out through the Alabama swamp lands and down the Lockport/Byron Rd. By the time we got there it was snowing lightly. Autry wheeled him around to see all the rooms and into the living room. I started to "lose it" for a while and had to get myself together out in the kitchen. I played Mom's organ a little for Dad and he had tears in his eyes. It was a bittersweet day. I'm so glad we brought him out. All we kids were there as well as some neighbors.

March 2

I tried to remember all the "little things" that were said here and there. So many times, whenever I did anything for Dad he would say, "Thank you, Dear." It just meant so much – not that I need a thank you, but it made me feel he was content and grateful. After sleeping late one morning, when he realized what time it was he said, "Farmers don't sleep this late!" Little things like these have put a smile on my face and is one of God's ways of strengthening my heart as Psalm 31:24 says, "Be of good courage, and He shall strengthen your heart, all ye that hope in the Lord."

I'm a little hesitant to even write the following, but it's one of those instances where you have to do what you have to do even when it's your own father. Since Dad was having more difficulty getting to the commode a nurse inserted a catheter one day. This isn't pleasant in the first place, and I know Dad didn't like it. However, during the second night, Dad must have pulled on it and he was in excruciating pain by the next morning which happened to be a Saturday. I called the hotline for visiting nurses to have them send someone as soon as possible. No one was available for some reason, but the one nurse I talked to said, "I can talk you through it – how to remove it." I didn't know what to say, perhaps just being in shock. Her next words: "Go get a pair of scissors!" "Scissors?" I asked. "Yes, scissors." I left Dad and ran into the dining room where I kept my scissors and returned and picked the phone back up, placing it on speaker, so I could listen and work! This was the hardest thing I ever had to do but Dad realized it had to be done and following her directions it really didn't take long and almost immediately, Dad wasn't in pain any longer. I said to him, "Well, Dad, you didn't know I was a doctor, too!" And we both had to laugh. (Actually, I wanted to cry). Some things are just plain hard to do when you are taking care of someone so close to you. But I was constantly reminded that God would always be there for me and He would help me through whatever I needed to do.

March 12

I didn't like what I saw this morning. Dad was weak. He needed to use the commode, but I couldn't get him to it. His legs had no strength, and he was like a dead weight. He was trying to stand but was falling against me. I had to use every ounce of my strength to push him back onto the bed. He was only partly on, but I ran and put my back support on before I hurt myself. I was finally able to get him partly onto the bed and resting once again.

Later, he had a spell. His arm went limp and his face blank and he didn't respond immediately when I asked him how he was. It took a few minutes and then I had a hard time getting him up higher on the bed. He also had blood coming out of a spot on his right eye. It's unreal how much he's gone down in only a few days. I did ask what kind of ice cream he'd like me to get next time; what was his favorite. He said, "Whatever kind you get is my favorite!" I find myself telling him, "I love you," often. Guess I just don't know when it will be the last one. He tells me the same and still says, "Thank you, Dear," all the time whenever I do anything.

March 13

After supper I read Dad a couple of chapters in Psalms (23 and 91). I talked about his salvation. He still remembers the day at Grace Baptist Church in Brockport when he trusted Christ as his Savior. He said, "Mom is in heaven." We talked about all of us being together again one day. The Lord had just impressed this upon me tonight – maybe the end is nearer than I think.

March 16

I was up 3 times in the night with Dad – twice just because of hearing him. He got the sheets and blankets all twisted once and was caught like a little cub bear. He said, "I can't do anything for myself. I think I'm getting close to the end. I've had a good life." You know what I did at that point; in fact, my whole day was emotionally draining.

Hospice did call. They are sending someone out tomorrow morning. But Dad's spirit has been up today. It's really been something. He's made me laugh several times. He asks for cider a lot, so I told him, "I'm going to have to change your name from the Chocolate Kid to the Cider Kid." He said, "You're going to make me drunk!" And when he drank it, he made a funny little move in bed and giggled!

Later in the evening I had a rough time getting him back to bed after using the commode. I used my knee on his behind to lift and direct him. We barely made it but we both plopped onto the side of the bed, and I said, "Well, Dad, we both made a safe landing!" Made us both laugh.

The Lord is so gracious because during the tears and heart aches today He has sent some precious little things to make us laugh and bring joy; that's just the way my Lord is and would you look at this verse! James 1:17 "Every good gift and every perfect gift is from above, and cometh down from the Father of lights." Thank you, Lord.

March 17

Nancy, from Hospice, came this morning – was here 3 hours. What an emotional day. I lost it several times and I knew Dad was hurting. She laid out everything as we all sat at the dining room table. Dad signed all the papers himself. He was worried about the cost; but it's all taken care of through Medicare and special funding for Hospice itself – even all the medicine will be taken care of. They will be sending in an aid 5 days a week for up to 3 hours a day. Don't know when she will start.

I fixed Dad lunch, but he didn't eat much at all; said he couldn't. I know it was because of the shock of hearing all this. He even said, "There's not much hope – I might as well give up – the sooner the better!" He did eat a fair supper, but only wants to sleep.

March 19

Dad had some company today. Before they left, he said, "I'm a very lucky man." He was referring to his family. Later in the evening I said to him, "Guess what I'm cooking for dinner tomorrow?" He thought a few seconds and said, "Wild rabbit, if you can catch it!" And he laughed after I burst out laughing. It was so cute.

March 21

When I went into Dad's room this morning, he was reaching out to the side of his head and asked, "Where's the bird?" Then he said, "Maybe I was dreaming." Maybe he was, but I'm just wondering if he is already starting that phase of seeing things. I'll have to watch.

March 23

What a taxing day this has been from get go! Dad had a problem even sitting up to eat breakfast. He started falling over so I laid him back and fed him, but he didn't eat much. Just when I was getting his bath ready, he said he needed to use the toilet, so I got him to the commode. It wasn't easy and it was also a mistake because he started leaning way over and I had to hold him from falling. The worst part was that he didn't have any strength to push up or even hang onto me. All I could do was pick him up and put him onto the bed and then pull everything up. I did a number on my back, but I put my back support on and I think it's okay (except it's hurting some tonight).

At supper he said he'd try to sit up again. He tried to work his fork and after getting a little food on it missed his mouth. I took over and gave him one bite and something happened. He didn't swallow, was shaking and started falling back. I called for Autry, and he helped me hold him until it looked like he finally swallowed, and we were able to get him back into a lying position. I fed him a little, mostly applesauce and chocolate pudding.

There's that verse again! "God is our refuge and strength, a very present help in trouble." Ps. 46:1. I couldn't have done it without Him.

March 25

Dad had some kind of seizure: his legs shook, arms went limp, color drained from his face and then his eyes stared upward; he didn't know we were there. I just held him for 2 to 3 minutes. We weren't sure he was coming back, but he finally did, and we got him settled in bed. He just seems to be slipping away. He is so weak. It was difficult bathing and dressing him today as he can't help much at all.

March 29

Throughout last night, Dad was calling my name. He isn't using the button on his stand anymore. Several times he was saying things that didn't make sense.

"Can someone get me out of here (my bed), I need to go to the toilet."

"The lights are all out; who's going to bring us our food down here?"

After several trips into his room, I finally grabbed my blanket and pillow and camped out on the recliner in the room. I was awake pretty much the whole night and got up with a tired, sick headache and just felt "out of it."

March 31

I stayed in the recliner again last night; got some sleep but it was broken. I gave Dad a relaxer and it helped some. He wasn't very responsive this morning, but I was able to spoon feed him some water and he did drink almost 4 ounces of instant breakfast. He seems to know who we are yet. He squeezes your hand, but we can't understand what he is trying to say anymore – that's hard.

Later in the day I took Dad's hand and said, "I'm here, Dad. It's Marlene and he faintly said, "I love you." At least that's what it sounded like and that's what I'll remember and cherish.

It was hard cooking supper and thinking, "Here we are eating, and I can't do anything for Dad."

I had picked up a prescription for liquid drops for pain and anxiety earlier. I had also given him drops for congestion earlier but held off on the new meds to see if he really needed them. By 12:00 I knew I had to give him something again and even though I hated the thought of morphine I gave him a minimal dose and the relaxer awhile later. He settled down and had a peaceful night. I, too, got a halfway decent sleep.

April 1

Dad is not responsive at all this morning. His breathing is fast and labored. He's running a temperature of over 102. He isn't squeezing my hand when I hold it. It was easier when I seemed to be able to do things for him. Now I can do nothing but be here for him—hold his hand, rub his arm or forehead, and tell him, "I love you and I'm here." But I guess that's a lot, too, and these are the most important things. He can remember them in heaven. It's not far away now. I've hated to even leave the room thinking something could happen the minute I leave. I've moved the recliner to beside his bed so I can just touch him and hold his hand even if I fall asleep. I just don't want to leave him alone. I want him to know I'm here.

April 2

I still think Dad knew I was here—kind of scared him once when I got down close and said, "This is Marlene, I'm here." He jumped a little. There may have been a little response from a few other things I said but nothing significant. I spent the remaining hours sitting in the recliner beside him and letting him know I was here. His facial color seems to have changed some – a more grayish look. Time almost seems at *a standstill. Our days are all numbered and only God knows when my dad's will be over.*

I kept looking at him and holding his hands. I love his hands and remember the song my son, Preston, sang at Mom and Dad's 50th anniversary about "These Hard-Working Hands." Well, his work is almost over—he'll be entering his rest soon. I managed to tell Dad today that I was a very lucky girl to have a dad like him and that I had the best Mom and Dad in the world. I hoped he could hear me.

I finished a conversation on the phone with my sister-in-law and hardly ten minutes later, as I was holding his hand, his breathing took an abrupt change. It was completely different from anything before. It was just as the "book" had described; "like a fish out of water." I immediately knew the end was here. Perhaps three minutes passed as I held him, kissed him, said, "I love you. It's alright to go—Jesus is waiting."

At 4:19 pm he took his last breath. There was no thrashing about or struggling—it was as if he was at peace—and I know he is—no more pain! Just think—Mom and Dad are together again.

Waiting for the ambulance and the man from the mortuary to come was so difficult. But the hardest was seeing them take Dad away and then go into the empty bedroom. I could hardly stand it. But God continued to give me more strength and more grace as there were still more difficult days ahead. The funeral took place sixteen years to the day after we had buried Mom.

BE STILL AND.....

> The Lord is so gracious because during the tears and heart aches today He has sent some precious little things to make us laugh and bring joy—but that's just the way my Lord is.

READ THE WORD

"He shall call upon me, and I will answer him: I will be with him in trouble; I will deliver him, and honor him. With long life will I satisfy him, and show him my salvation."
Ps. 91:15,16

HIDE THE WORD

"Yea, though I walk through the valley of the shadow of death, I will fear no evil; for thou art with me; thy rod and thy staff they comfort me."
Ps. 23:4

PRAY THE WORD

Dear Father, Thank you for blessing my father with a long life. and thank You for being with me as I helped him walk through the valley of the shadow of death. There have been tears and heartaches but also times of joy; and now there is joy, because I know he is in Your presence, and I will see him again. Amen

KNOW THAT I AM GOD

Psalm 46:10

RETIREMENT

During our almost 9 years in Niagara Falls, Autry had several heart issues. He had more stents placed in his heart, but he also had his second open heart surgery. During our last year there I could see his health deteriorating more and more and he, too, realized that he wasn't going to be able to continue preaching and leading a church. He would retire sooner than he wanted to.

Retirement! Brings all kinds of pictures to your mind, doesn't it? Changes – some big, some small; but changes; and change doesn't come easily to us. It takes us out of our comfort zone.

For us, the first thing retirement brought was a major move; selling our home in Niagara Falls, which we could no longer afford, and moving some 200 miles into another state, to live with our son, Lyle, and his family. We were grateful for the lower apartment they provided in their three-story home. A brand-new kitchen with a picture window letting in the sun's warmth and cheerfulness; and a newly remodeled bathroom made our living situation very comfortable and enjoyable. Before moving there, we set up an apartment in the basement of his parent's home in Batavia, NY, as we knew one day we would get that call from them needing our help to take care of them. So, we knew all of this was only temporary. Neither of us looked forward to another move, but since Autry was their only child, we knew this is what we would have to do and what God would want us to do. We just didn't know when.

It was great being around our son and daughter-in-law and our 3 grandchildren: one in junior high and two senior high students.

"Grandma's Café" on Saturday mornings was a hit. I printed out menus on Friday evenings for all family members to check what they wanted for breakfast the following morning: anything from pancakes, French toast, eggs, sausage, bacon, toast (choice of bread), coffee, juice; all made to order! Our time together on these mornings was something we'll all cherish. My grandson, Shane (who has Down Syndrome) would always stay downstairs and help me clean up. One of his favorite things following breakfast was singing, "Sunshine on my shoulders makes me _____, and he'd wait for me to squeak out "happy" in a silly tone; and we'd both laugh.

My relationship with Shane was very special. He loved to walk with me in a nearby cemetery. The cemetery was beautiful with paved walkways, little hills and flowers. All kinds of tall trees graced the grounds and flowering bushes with their awesome fragrances were a delight. At one point Shane would decide to take a path different from mine. His goal was to try to beat me back to the car. A stop for ice cream afterwards was not uncommon.

Shane loved to copy me in different ways from repeating something I'd say, sniffing or coughing, or sighing and he'd laugh thinking he was so funny. I love his laugh.

But one of the most special things I did with him was help with his reading. I had him read some simple stories and I made up easy worksheets for him to answer some questions about the story. I did the same with Bible stories. After all these years, he still remembers his favorite with Shadrach, Meshach, and Abednego in the fiery furnace. And when asked about the fourth person in the furnace with them, he still answers, "Jesus." His favorite verse, which he will turn to in his Bible, is Deuteronomy 6:5 "Thou shalt love the Lord thy God with all your heart, and with all your soul, and with all your might." Using my children's book that I wrote, "Grandma Tell Me the Easter Story," I was able to lead him to the Lord. And then through a worksheet I created, I helped him understand what baptism means and we were able to watch as he followed the Lord into the waters of baptism.

Now that I live 4 hours away, phone calls are always welcome, and he will usually ask, "When are you coming to visit?" It's never too soon for him.

Autry and I also found a small church to attend while we were there. This was the first one since he had retired. I had a hard time getting used to "listening" to a new pastor, and even calling him my pastor. After all, for 30 years Autry was "my pastor!" But we did get involved as Autry taught a men's Bible class and I taught a ladies' Bible class. I played the piano often as well as the organ and I started and led a choir. Music was always my love, so this was very special to me. We had adjusted nicely to our "new life."

What is taking you "out of your comfort zone" if you are at this stage in life? Less income, a necessary move, boredom, feeling unneeded? Sometimes it isn't even retirement that brings changes; but something else like health issues and we are so good at being "worry warts!" God has a lot to say about worrying, but He also has some things to say about contentment. We can choose to be miserable in our retirement days or we can choose to be content. Remember… happiness depends on our circumstances, but we can have the joy of the Lord in spite of our circumstances. **Retirement can be a huge, dreaded cloud** over one's life. But let God take you through it. He wants you to live an abundant life. John 10:10b says, "I am come that you might have life and that you might have it more abundantly."

BE STILL AND.....

> Retirement! Brings all kinds of pictures to your mind, doesn't it? Changes – some big, some small, but none the less, changes; and change doesn't come easily to us. It takes us out of our comfort zones.

READ THE WORD

"Therefore, do not worry, saying 'What shall we eat? or 'What shall we drink? or 'What shall we wear?' For after all these things the Gentiles seek. For your heavenly Father knows that you need all these things. But seek ye first the kingdom of God and His righteousness, and all these things shall be added to you. Therefore do not worry about tomorrow, for tomorrow will worry about its own things. Sufficient for the day is its own trouble."
Matt. 6:31-34

HIDE THE WORD

"...for I have learned in whatever state I am, to be content."
Phil. 4:11b

PRAY THE WORD

Dear Father, It's so easy for me to worry about so many different things. Help me to be content no matter what kind
of needs I have. You know what
they all are, and you will take care of me as
you do even the birds of the air.
So, help me not to worry but to seek You and your righteousness.
That's what is important. Amen.

KNOW THAT I AM GOD

Psalm 46:10

FROM A DUNGEON TO A PALACE

After four and a half years the day came – the phone call we knew we would get one day. "Can you come? We need your help?" The call from his parents! I must admit it was the call I was dreading to get. **It was that cloud** that had been looming ahead of us for some time, but now we were about to enter it.

I had prayed for God's strength and grace for just this time, and I tried to prepare myself emotionally. I knew what the basement looked like – it was dark, damp, cold, with only two small windows which you couldn't see out because of bushes. It would always be night down there and we'd have to have lights on throughout the day. My attitude – not good – I had already called it my "Dungeon Apartment." God had been preparing me for this move, too, although I didn't realize it at the time. Before we left our church family in PA, I had been teaching a ladies' Bible Class and had completed a study on contentment – how timely! How many times had I told them and encouraged those dear ladies in this area of contentment that we (I) can choose to be miserable in my circumstances or I can choose to be content and accept whatever God allows in my life; knowing that He is sovereign and will give me the grace and strength to face and go through whatever God daily places in my life.

So, I had a choice to make. I could remain miserable, unhappy, and depressed, or I could choose to let God transform my heart and my attitude. As I placed furniture, and arranged family pictures, a tapestry, figurines, candles, an oriental carpet, dishes, etc. God did change my heart. Oh, it was still dark down there, but my attitude: I no longer called it my dungeon apartment but "my little palace."

As God was working in my own heart, I often thought about the many people who are living in dungeons of their own making. They don't have the glorious light of the Lord Jesus Christ shining in their lives. The darkness of their sin, their fears, their loss of health, family trials, financial needs and so many other things have them chained and trapped in their own dungeons. People are looking in the wrong direction for their contentment. They think things—favorable circumstances, a nice home, good job, are what they need. The fact is contentment does not come in anything, but a Person and that Person is Jesus Christ.

I think of Paul and Silas singing "in a dungeon" and their glorious release which resulted in a man trusting the Lord as his Savior. We, too, can choose to sing and praise God in our darkest dungeon. God can and will change our hearts and attitudes **and take us out of those clouds of darkness**; take us from the very pit of hell to the glorious heights of heaven. And we know that one day we will be transformed, and we will live with Him forever in our palace in Heaven. Hallelujah!

BE STILL AND…..

> As God was working in my own heart, I often thought about the many people who are living in dungeons of their own making. People are looking in the wrong direction for their contentment. Contentment does not come in anything, but a Person and that Person is Jesus Christ.

READ THE WORD

"Let not your heart be troubled: you believe in God, believe also in me. In my Father's house are many mansions: if it were not so I would have told you. I go to prepare a place for you. And if I go and prepare a place for you, I will come again, and receive you unto myself, that where I am, there you may be also.
John 14:1-3

HIDE THE WORD

"Sirs, what must I do to be saved? And they said, Believe, on the Lord Jesus Christ, and thou shall be saved."
Acts 16:31

PRAY THE WORD

Dear Father, I feel like I am in a dungeon of my own making. Forgive me, for I am your child. Help me to sing and praise your holy name in spite of my circumstances. Use me to reach others for you; and don't let me forget that I have a mansion waiting for me in glory where I will be with you forever. Amen

KNOW THAT I AM GOD

Psalm 46:10.

NOW THAT HE'S GONE

Autry enjoyed spending time with his dad. His dad had built a large woodworking shop in the backyard, and they would spend hours creating their masterpieces. Both were very talented in that area. Friday evenings the four of us would enjoy a fish fry at Town 'n Country. Otherwise, the evening meals were prepared by me.

Autry's dad's stamina grew less and less as time went on and Autry also was having more issues with his heart and would tire easily. Their hours in the shop together slowly disappeared. (It is still one of the saddest things for me to do –walk into that large shop and see all the machinery sitting there— silent!). It was only a little over a year and a half before Autry's health took a turn for the worse and he **departed this life the day after Christmas, December 26, 2013. (You'll find this in the section Till Death do us Part).**

I hope no one ever says to you when you have lost your loved one, "It's going to be okay; in time you'll get over it." No, it's not okay; no, you aren't going to get over it. Yes, it will get better, but it will never be the same again. Your whole life is different, and that's what we have to live with. That's reality! Grieving is a journey – but a journey you can walk through with the Lord Jesus Christ. It's wonderful when your loved one knows the Lord and you know they are in heaven. But we don't need to hear someone say, "You shouldn't grieve; you'll see him again. He's better off." You have to realize that sometimes people just don't know what to say. Unless they have gone through it, they have no idea what's going on inside us. They expect us to "be better" in a matter of months. Yes, we can have joy in the fact that we'll see them again; but in the meantime, we are still down here living without them. It's not easy!

Over the next three to four years, I not only was trying to deal with grief, but I would have three more surgeries: two shoulder repairs and my second hip replacement. (My first hip replacement was done just 8 months before Autry passed away). I believe most were related in some way to me being the caregiver for Ma & Pa (my in-laws). For close to a year, I dealt with sciatic pain which went down my right leg. Walking was bad enough, but trying to sit down and be comfortable didn't come easy and getting back up was another story. Living with pain can be so consuming. All you want is relief in some way. I couldn't tolerate most pain medications as I was allergic to them, or they made me like a zombie! So, there was little relief. Many times, I prayed and asked God to take it away, but He had other plans, at least for some time. I came to realize the Bible is better than any pain reliever. Even though my body wasn't working the way I would like it to, I could be satisfied and content even when I was hurting. I realized God was using this in my life and He wanted to use all of this to mold me to become more like Christ. But it would be up to my **choosing** to let Him do so. Rather than focusing on my pain, I needed to focus on my Savior and focus on the Word.

I thought of Paul's "thorn in the flesh," and how God didn't remove it even though he had prayed and asked God to take it away. What did Paul say? *"For this thing I besought the Lord thrice, that it might depart from me. And he said unto me, my grace is sufficient for thee: for my strength is made perfect in weakness. Most gladly therefore will I rather glory in my infirmities, that the power of Christ may rest upon me. Therefore, I take pleasure in infirmities, in reproaches, in necessities, in persecutions, in distresses for Christ's sake: for when I am weak, then am I strong."* II Cor. 12:8-10

And of course, there's Jesus. Oh, how He suffered for me. *"For even hereunto were you called: because Christ also suffered for us, leaving us an example, that you should follow his steps; Who did no sin, neither was guile found in his mouth: who, when he was reviled, reviled not again; when he suffered, he threatened not; but committed himself to him that judges righteously. Who his own self bare our sins in his own body on the tree; that we, being dead to sins, should live unto righteousness; by whose stripes you were healed" I Pet. 2:21-24.*

My pain was nothing in comparison to what my Lord and Savior suffered. But it was a great reminder to never take for granted what He went through to purchase my redemption.

Jesus' goal was always to live to please the Father in the good times as well as the hard times. That's what I decided I wanted to do. I wrote the following on an index card and placed it on my nightstand so I could see it every morning:

PLEASING

GOD

IS THE GOAL!

On the back side I wrote:

This is what Christ did –

Lived to please the Father

(IN BOTH THE HARD TIMES AND THE GOOD TIMES!)

God never promised a life on a bed of roses. But He did promise that He would go with us and never forsake us. He is our resource, our refuge, our strength, and our hope. *"The Lord is my rock, and my fortress, and my deliverer; my God, my strength, in whom I will trust" Ps. 18:2.*

We (I) had choices to make every day. I needed to choose what I didn't like for God to be able to use it in my life to grow me and make me into what He wanted me to be. God's word was vital in my life; that's where my focus needed to be. ***"This is my comfort in my affliction: for your word has given me life" Ps. 119:50.*** And that's where my comfort came from.

One of my favorite scripture passages I found myself reading over and over again when my pain seemed unbearable is II Cor. 4:16-18. It reminded me that I have something far better to look forward to; oh, not in this life, but in the life to come. And considering eternity, any suffering we (I) go through is only for a moment. It says:

"For which cause we faint not; but though our outward man perish, yet the inward man is renewed day by day. For our light affliction, which is but for a moment, worketh for us a far more exceeding and eternal weight of glory; While we look not at the things which are seen, but at the things which are not seen: for the things which are seen are temporal; but the things which are not seen are eternal."

May I encourage you, dear readers, not to give up when you are going through health or other difficult situations. Stay focused. Trust God and press on: ***"I press toward the mark for the prize of the high calling of God in Christ Jesus" Phil. 3:14. It*** will be worth it all. ***"But rejoice, inasmuch as you are partakers of Christ's sufferings; that, when his glory shall be revealed, you may be glad also with exceeding joy" I Pet. 4:13.***

BE STILL AND.....

> My pain was nothing in comparison to what my Lord and Savior suffered. But it was a great reminder to never take for granted what He went through to purchase my redemption.

READ THE WORD

"For this thing I besought the Lord thrice, that it might depart from me. And he said unto me, My grace is sufficient for thee: for my strength is made perfect in weakness. Most gladly therefore will I rather glory in my infirmities, that the power of Christ may rest upon me. Therefore, I take pleasure in infirmities, in reproaches, in necessities, in persecutions, in distresses for Christ's sake: for when I am weak, then am I strong."
II Cor. 12:8-10

HIDE THE WORD

"For which cause we faint not; but though our outward man perish, yet the inward man is renewed day by day. For our light affliction, which is but for a moment, worketh for us a far more exceeding and eternal weight of glory; While we look not at the things which are seen, but at the things which are not seen: for the things which are seen are temporal; but the things which are not seen are eternal."
II Cor. 4:16-18

PRAY THE WORD

Dear Father, I thank you for the pain I am feeling at this moment. I don't understand the "why", but I know you are using it for a purpose in my life. I also realize that this isn't going to last forever; it will pass; if not in this lifetime the next; and I look forward to what You have ahead for me in eternity. Amen

KNOW THAT I AM GOD

Psalm 46:10

CARE GIVING – 24/7 FOR MY IN-LAWS

(Part 1)

I believe my grieving process was delayed and lengthened because I had so much responsibility taking care of my in-laws that I didn't have time to grieve the way I should have for my husband. Autry was their only child and we both had agreed we would be the ones to take care of his parents in their old age. Of course, now Autry was gone; but I chose to stay and care for them. I kept a combination of a diary/journal on my in-laws during this time. The following are excerpts from my writing and will take you through some of the days on my journey in that season of my life. (I called my in-laws Ma and Pa.)

July 27, 2015

    Ma and Pa are still able to get their own breakfast and lunch (actually, mostly Pa). I'm fixing supper every night and Sunday dinner except when they or the three of us go out. I do all the cleaning and most of the grocery shopping. They do the laundry—Pa helps a lot with that, too. Pa has fallen four or five times—getting harder to get up and is more and more unsteady on his feet. His memory also seems to be steadily getting worse. He is very forgetful. Last night he came downstairs and asked, "What's today?" I said Sunday. He thought it was Monday and had even argued with Ma about it. He really looked confused. Ma did fall once in the bathroom and fortunately I heard her calling, "Jack," from my room. He wasn't home and I, somehow, was able to help her up. She is very impatient with Pa as he doesn't hear her. That is getting worse all the time, too; plus she either speaks so low or talks from another room and he can't hear her! Pa is using a cane more since I told him he needed to do that, and Ma uses her walker. She is extremely slow; shuffles a lot and is very bent over.

I obviously don't know what lies ahead and I just try to take one day at a time praying for wisdom, strength, grace to do whatever, and that I will be loving, kind, merciful, and patient. God has brought me to this situation for a reason and I know He will not fail me. He will see me through to the end.

September 14

Two more months have gone by. Some things remain about the same, others seem to be deteriorating. I must keep reminding myself it's still their home, they have ways of doing things or not doing things and I just have to try and ignore it. But it's not always easy.

I can't clean like I'd like to, and the clutter is getting worse. They just plain seem to be getting messier – the kitchen table, even the floor and more issues in the bathroom! I really don't think Pa is bathing like he should (still don't know what I should or shouldn't say about that).

Pa has lost another cane – misplaced two in one day! His legs are getting weaker. He has gotten up several nights thinking it was the next day and even shaved, etc. On Saturday, he thought it was Monday. I have started leaving him notes on the kitchen table to remind him to do something. And driving the car – I should say "NOT" driving the car is an issue coming sooner than I want it to. I am getting more concerned in that area. This is going to be VERY difficult.

I just keep asking the Lord for strength, wisdom, and grace and take one day at a time. I also ask that the fruit of the Spirit be evident in my life as I care for them.

November 10

Ma messed up on some pills. On Tuesday morning the morning pills were already gone, her nighttime ones were still there, but Wednesday mornings were also gone! And she had no idea what or when she took them. She just said, "Well, they didn't kill me!"

Pa doesn't remember me telling him where I would be or what I was going to be doing. He still has to "hunt" for his cane often. He is more unstable getting up from the table. He says he gets dizzier since the doctor changed his pills. Not sure what to think. Ma fell in the evening on the kitchen floor. After asking her some questions, she said she thinks she just went down, legs gave way! She lay there 20 to 30 minutes before we could get her up and sit on her walker.

November 15

Ma couldn't walk or stand. Pa managed to get her onto the walker again and brought her to the table. She struggled getting from it to the chair.

November 16

Ma still can't walk. She says she can "hobble" some on one leg, but also said, "It'll go away!" I'm not so sure. And Pa, I think, just doesn't want to accept reality. When we talked about getting her out the door for appointments, he said, "She'll have to help some!" Well, right now there is no "help some."

January 2, 2016

Pa went to Walmart. I couldn't leave Ma today. I gave him a list of 2 things to get: 1) Fiber One Cereal 2) Pick up Ma's prescription. He thought there should have been 2 prescriptions, and he never did get the right cereal; came home with 2 large boxes of the wrong kind, plus 6 or more cans of Spam! Plus, he got lost in the store AGAIN and then couldn't find his car AGAIN! He did get help from someone.

April 9

Not a whole lot of change but the memory of both is getting worse. She has been messing up on medications and Pa came up with the idea for him to put each time slot of pills into a medicine bottle and give it to her. Sounded good but he was doing it wrong!

Ma has no interest in anything. She gets dressed only when she has an appointment and I know she is not getting into the shower. She did once recently but that was the first time in a long time. Pa still isn't changing his clothes (outer) much either. I don't know how to handle some of this. Pa is also having difficulty writing checks and I may have to take over completely in that area soon. He has asked for help several times.

They both had a checkup at their primary care doctor. Ma got upset when a few things were said about her trying to do some more chores at home. Her comment, "Guess I need to get a new doctor, a new husband, and a new daughter-in-law!" Wow! That's twice now I've heard something like that. It kind of makes me nervous, but again I must let it go and realize she may not even know what she is saying and yet I know she simply doesn't like to be told to do anything.

July 10

Just in the last month Pa seems to be going down fast. The memory is bad, but it's more than that. He looks like he is losing weight, he is more unsteady on his feet. He said he thinks it's because he can't "feel his feet!" His appetite isn't good anymore - says he's not hungry most of the time. He has no energy; can hardly take care of bathing Satin, their dog, anymore! (Not good). He sleeps into the mornings and going back to bed more often and earlier at night. The bathroom issues with him are getting worse.

With my own surgery 4 weeks ago on my shoulder, I've had to resort to TV dinners and cleaning the best I can for a while. I still get frustrated with that because of the clutter all over, but it is what it is! Just one day at a time! Plus, I'm doing all the bills now. Pa gave me his checkbook as he was making too many mistakes. I do BOTH of their medicines now, too. He gave up on that as he realized he wasn't doing things right. But Ma has still messed up on some pills – taking them out of the wrong slot and not remembering doing it! I told her about it and said, "I'm sorry, I don't mean to be a pain, I am just trying to help you." Her comment: "That's okay, I'll let you be a pain!" Had to laugh – what are you going to do!

September 24

After spending a total of 8 hours between a doctor's visit and being sent to the ER for several tests, the verdict is not good. CT showed 9cm mass on Pa's left kidney and several lesions in his lungs. More appointments were scheduled.

I feel like I'm getting ready to start another chapter in my life (in reality, in all 3 of our lives).

August 4

Pa has lost 22 pounds. The mass is fast moving, and we were told, "There is no cure, but there may be some things that can be done to keep him comfortable."

August 5

Pa sleeps most of the day. His appetite is all but gone; he seems to be getting thinner and weaker every day. The bathroom issues are getting worse and worse. For several days supper is the only meal he has eaten. I bought him Ensure and some yogurt.

August 22

After waiting a couple of weeks, we finally had an appointment at Strong Hospital in Rochester. Meeting with the oncologist pretty much laid everything out for us. Pa has Stage 4 Kidney Cancer, and it is spreading rapidly; even into his lungs. They will not be operating.

September 2

As the three of us were sitting in the living room Pa kept looking at Ma and finally said, "I love you, Bertie," and she answered back, "I love you!" I've never heard either one of them say that before. I about lost it.

September 3

Ma went into the bedroom to wake Pa up in the afternoon, but just stood looking at him and came back down the hallway almost wailing! It was pitiful. I hugged her and tried to console her. I don't know if it finally hit her or what. She asked, "What am I going to do without Jack?"

September 9

Hospice came this morning and I had to sign a bunch of papers. They will call next week and set up a schedule for the nurse to come. Pa keeps telling me, "Thank you, Marlene for everything." I've had to hide tears several times. He's something else and his sense of humor is still there.

September 13

The nurse from Hospice came. She got Pa into the shower - yeah! She and I changed the sheets and pads. She said to me that Ma is having as many or more issues as Pa and hopes more help will be available for me.

September 26

Pa fell in the bathroom. He tried to walk without the walker and went down between the toilet and the vanity. I got the trash can out from under him, but I had to call Hospice and then 911. Two paramedics came and got him up – nothing was broken.

September, 30

I have been sleeping in the bedroom next to theirs for several nights now, so I can help more. He has fallen over onto the bed several times and it is very difficult for me to get him situated in bed. Early this morning there was a crash. Somehow, he managed to walk out into the hallway, and crashed against my bedroom door as he fell to the floor. Once again it was a call to 911.

October 2

Pa doesn't think to call me with the bell I've had in his room for some time. He doesn't want to "bother" me. But I've had a baby monitor going for some time and I keep it as near me as possible wherever I am. This also makes it harder for me to sleep as I hear everything. And tonight was BAD! He got confused, talked all night (not coherently), saw things all night long. There literally was no sleeping as the dog also barked whenever I was ready to doze off. I know she senses what is happening.

October 4

A friend came and stayed with Pa while I went to a checkup appointment on my shoulder with my orthopedic doctor. He plain out told me I can't be pushing or pulling on a wheelchair or lifting and doing all the things that I've had to do with Pa. It's only been 4 months since my shoulder surgery, and I could really do damage. I know this is true, but it is also hard to swallow.

Returning home, the Hospice nurse was here. We talked. I realized I can't keep taking care of Pa anymore. I just don't have the strength. I explained to Pa the best I could that I couldn't keep doing what I had been because it was really not good on my own body. I told him I never wanted to have to talk about this, but my doctor is insisting. He understood.

The possibility of getting Pa into Crossroads Home was brought up. This is an end-of-life facility hardly a mile and a half from us. I know the lady who runs it. They had one opening. She came and by the end of the day all paperwork was done and approved for Pa to go there tomorrow! One question she asked Pa was, "How long do you think you have before you leave this life?" He answered, "One week."

The next several days are almost a blur. Ma and I spent as much time with him as we could. There were times when Pa held her hand. I was so glad. Ma needed that. The volunteers at Crossroads are wonderful. They are doing everything they can to keep Pa comfortable, but all the signs are there; he will soon leave this old world.

October 10 *(my birthday)*

I was up early and went over to Crossroads. Pa didn't have the strength to drink through a straw, so the nurse used a dropper for some water and a little Boost. He wasn't very alert, but I was able to say, "I love you," and he softly replied, "I love you, too." He said that at least twice today. I told him it was okay to go and see Jesus and his son, Autry. He shook his head. I told him I'd take care of Ma and he didn't have to worry about that. I'm just really asking the Lord that it will be soon. I hate to see him this way.

Ma and I stayed overnight as the volunteers thought this would be the night. One volunteer softly sang, "Amazing Grace" in his ear. This wasn't the night.

October 11

After being with Pa all day yesterday, Ma and I were pretty much exhausted ourselves. After ordering supper, I decided to run home and get some more things that we might need. It took me longer than I thought and only minutes before I got back, Pa was ushered into eternity. I totally lost it. I was so angry at myself for having left. I cried so hard it made my chest literally hurt. Everyone said not to beat myself up, but I couldn't help it. I had been caring for him for weeks (months), and literally 24/7 and then for him to pass away while I was gone that little while was awful! But later, I realized he just didn't want me to have to go through those final moments seeing him taking those last few breaths. His departure to heaven was at 7:15 pm. He has met his Savior, and I'm sure has already seen his son, my husband, Autry! (Pa was at Crossroads House for exactly 1 week!)

These were days of **breaking through many dark clouds.** Caregiving is draining; not only physically, but emotionally. Every day I asked the Lord for strength, wisdom, and grace, and learned to take just one day at a time. One thing I tried to work on was to praise the Lord even in the hard times. I had also asked God that the fruit of the Spirit would be evident in my life as I took care of my in-laws. Once in a while I would receive hurtful remarks, mostly from my mother-in-law; but I had to let them go and realize she may not even have known what she was saying. But other times, there were remarks like, "Thank you, Marlene for everything." I really knew they appreciated my help.

The other big thing God helped me to accept that I needed to break through was admitting my own limitations. This was so vital. Placing Pa in that "end stage" facility about killed me, but for my own health's sake it was necessary. We can't beat ourselves up when we have to make a decision like this. God knows our hearts and He also knows our limitations and doesn't expect us to cause harm to our own bodies. We must learn to take care of our own physical needs, or we won't be able to help anyone. Above all – Stay in the Word! That's where my strength and encouragement came from. And He wasn't finished yet. There was more to come.

BE STILL AND.....

Care-giving is draining; not only physically, but emotionally. Every day I asked the Lord for strength, wisdom, and grace, and learned to take just one day at a time.

READ THE WORD

"I will bless the Lord at all times: his praise shall continually be in my mouth. O taste and see that the LORD is good: blessed is the man that trusts in Him."
Psalm 34:1, 8

HIDE THE WORD

"God is our refuge and strength, a very present help in trouble. Psalm 46:1

PRAY THE WORD

Dear Father, I thank you for the physical strength that you gave me while caring for my father-in-law. I praise you that you allowed me to be able to take care of him for as long as I did. Amen.

KNOW THAT I AM GOD

Psalm 46:10

CARE GIVING – 24/7 FOR MY IN-LAWS

(Part 2)

November 4

I can't remember all that went on each day of the last few weeks. I've just been exhausted. It took me several days to feel like I was somewhat rested. I had a list of things I'd been working on. The paperwork and financial things at the bank have been overwhelming.

November 25

Ma isn't happy with any of the aides, nurses and therapists that have been coming to the house to help. She has made some of them go away. The physical therapist was able to get her to do a few things but when that time was up, she didn't follow through with anything. Several times I've tried to get her up, but she often says, "No," and has added, "I don't feel good," and "I don't care!" She told one nurse, "Everyone tries to tell me I should get up and try to walk more. You can tell me that, but I won't do it!" And that's just how it is. She'll do what she wants and that's it!

January 14, 2017

I thought I was going to have to call 911. I went to bed late, around 11:30, and Ma was sitting at the kitchen table still looking at the Penny Saver I gave her after supper. At 12:00 I went back out – she was still at the table with the paper and said she would come to bed after she finished her pop from supper. 1:00, still up, but struggling at the doorway with her walker, and fiddling with the light switches. I watched as she groaned with every step down the hallway having an awful time walking. It was after 1:30 before she made it to her side of the bed. At 4:45, I heard, "Jack! Jack! Help me! I need help!" I went in and there she was – half crunched on the bed; her legs stretched out with no strength to push onto the bed. I couldn't lift her – tried to push and keep her feet from sliding. I finally got shoes on her and "eventually" she was able to get enough traction to inch her way onto the bed. It was a long process. There was very little sleep for me that night as I was up a little after 6:00 am.

January 15

While eating my dinner I heard, "Marlene, Marlene!" There she was again, crunched on the bed, legs dangling. I finally got her back in bed. She said she didn't feel right and probably should get checked out. I called some friends for some help, and we were able to get her into her wheelchair, out to my car and finally into ER. It didn't take them long to give us the prognosis. She'd had a stroke!

January 18

Ma has been transported for rehab to the LeRoy Village Greens. Medicare will cover at least 2 months of the financial cost.

Over the next 2 months, the staff was dealing with some of the same things I was doing while she was still home. She didn't like to have to get up for her therapy session, or even for breakfast and spoke rather harshly (to say the least) to those trying to help her. She just wanted to be "left alone."

I still wrestled with the idea of bringing her back home. I had promised Pa I would take care of her, and I already felt terrible that she had to be in this nursing facility for rehab. I decided I would TRY to bring her home and I started to get things in order for this to happen. I even had a ramp built on the front porch so I would be able to get her into the house. There would be no other way to get her in. I made all kinds of calls trying to line up wheelchair transportation. I went to the Genesee County Nursing home in Batavia regarding their adult day care program. It seemed great, but I didn't know if she would qualify or even want to go.

It seemed when Ma started hearing about coming home, she became a little more agreeable about doing rehab and yet there were still days she refused. I wrestled with all kinds of feelings and emotions. My *"famous"* words; *"I just don't know what to think! Can I handle it? I dread it. I don't know what the Lord really wants me to do. Will she just resort to going back to bed most of the day?"*

The nursing home had agreed to let me take her home for a trial run for a weekend and see how things would go. They held her room (just in case)! They knew, but I still had to try.

A cousin of my husband's helped me get her into my car and up the ramp. We still struggled getting the wheelchair through the doorway. But she was home! It wasn't long at all before the disaster struck. The bowel issues hit like a ton of bricks. I spent an hour and a half getting her and all the bedding cleaned up. I already felt my lower back hurting as well as my shoulder and left leg! She was just plain too heavy for me to handle. I felt the Lord was showing me the same thing that He did when I was caring for Pa. He was showing me my limitations. I just needed to get her home that weekend to open my eyes to the plain facts: I can't do it, and it has nothing to do with wanting or not wanting to do it or with depending on the Lord. Yes, He is my strength, but my body is saying, "No!" I had been praying that the Lord would show me in some definite way which direction to go. He did. It was very similar to what He showed me when I was caring for Pa. He let me know when I could no longer care for him. I toughed out the weekend, but Monday morning we headed back to the nursing home. I continued to visit 4 times a week finding she was getting weaker, and still telling aids to "leave her alone!"

By now finances were used up through Medicare and monthly payments were set up. Not a pretty picture!

May 4

My kids and I started talking about bringing her home again. Of course, all of us know that I could not do it alone. My oldest son, Preston, and daughter-in-law Tracy, were in a transition point with their jobs and they were willing to come and live with me to help me care for Ma. Once again, there were a lot of things to do to get ready for this "adventure."

Tracy and I made a good team, and my son was a life saver helping to turn her or pull her up higher on the bed. But all the issues she had before were only getting worse. She's getting weaker and not eating or drinking much. I read to her a couple of my devotions from my book, "A Daily Walk with God" and talked about heaven. She said she wants to go see Pa. Her eyes seem a little glossy and her left arm is very weak. Caring for her is super hard with her just lying there.

May 11

Hospice came and I did all the paperwork. It was obvious Ma was now in the end stage of life.

From this point on, we never knew what to expect every day. We might be told to "get lost and leave me alone," or she would be pleasant. There were days she only wanted to be in bed and then there were days we were able to get her into her wheelchair and she'd come out into the kitchen and eat with us. She seemed glad her grandson and Tracy were here. On Memorial Day, we had her outside for the first time in months to enjoy a picnic with several of my family who were visiting. She was excited about that.

As the end drew near there were some nights we stayed with her thinking, "This was the time." One evening as we sat with her, we told her it was okay to go. Her breathing was shallow and there was no

response. But all of a sudden, she turned over by herself and was totally alert! It was only a matter of a day or so and she, as Pa had done, began seeing people and often called out, "Mama."

We were able to keep her comfortable with morphine, and she quietly passed into eternity in the middle of the night on **June 25***. She was truly home now. Home in heaven and with Pa and Autry and of course, Jesus.*

God continued to help me **break through all those clouds associated with care-giving**. I learned so much (about myself) and saw just how big my God was. Nothing is impossible with Him. I learned that when I needed help, I didn't need to be afraid to ask for it. When I needed a break for a few hours or even a few days, I could find someone who could fill in for me. I wasn't a super person who could do everything on my own. I needed help physically, but again my spiritual help came from the Lord and His word. Oh, what a great God I have!

Breaking Through the Clouds

BE STILL AND.....

I had been praying that the Lord would show me in some definite way which direction to go. He did. It was very similar to what He showed me when I was caring for Pa.

READ THE WORD

"Trust in the Lord with all your heart; lean not unto your own understanding. In all your ways acknowledge Him and he shall direct your path."
Prov. 3:5, 6

HIDE THE WORD

"Death is swallowed up in victory. O death, where is thy sting? O grave, where is thy victory? The sting of death is sin; and the strength of sin is the law. But thanks be to God, which gives us the victory through our Lord Jesus Christ."
I Cor. 15:54c - 57

PRAY THE WORD

Dear Father, I am so grateful for the way You have led in my care for my in-laws. And now, I know they are in Your presence, and I will see them again, too, because "death, where is thy sting?" Amen.

KNOW THAT I AM GOD

Psalm 46:10

ALONE—BUT OH, SO NOT ALONE

I always felt that my grieving was in stages. After Autry was gone, I still had my mother and father-in-law, as I was living with and busy taking care of them 24/7. When my father-in-law passed away, I still had my mother-in-law, and the care went on. When she passed, I still had my son, Preston and daughter-in-law, Tracy (who had been helping me care for Ma) with me for another 4 months. They had decided to stay with me and help with some remodeling my kids thought I should do. But when they left, I was now alone. And it hit me hard.

For almost five years I had been living in the basement, my husband with me for one and a half of those years. Now I was moving from the basement to the main part of the home; but we had never lived together up there. Oh, yes, we often ate up there with my in-laws, but that wasn't our home together. Our home was in the basement. It took me a long time to consider it "my home." That was partly why my children wanted me to do some remodeling. I loved my new kitchen; and little by little as I had painting done throughout the house, purchased some new furniture and just rearranged things, I finally could call it my home. Remember? The basement was dark! Now I had light; windows to look out. For weeks, every morning after I got up, I would just stand looking out the large dining room window into my spacious back yard with the birds at the feeders and cry; and just thank the Lord for His blessings and for all His care for me.

I almost felt useless at times because my days weren't filled up with caring for anyone. Some days I just felt empty. Once again, I knew I had to be careful. It would be so easy to have pity parties or fall into depression.

I continued to write my Monday morning blogs for my website and I prayed that the Lord would open doors of ministry for me and show me what He wanted me to do. Phone calls would come off and on asking me if I could speak at a lady's luncheon or banquet. Then I had breakfast with our pastor's wife one morning. She suggested that I put together material for a workshop related to widows and other losses, as my life had been so full of different losses. I began to pray and ask for the Lord's help in putting my thoughts together. I realized just how much God had brought me through, the comfort He had given me, and the things that He taught me. Perhaps I could now share this with others on their journey of grief. I developed a workshop for widows but then expanded it to cover all losses which I titled, **"There's Life after Loss."**

You don't "get over" grief. Yes, it will get better, but it never will be the same; your whole life is different, and that's what we must live with. That's what I'm living with. That's reality! Someone said to me, "You are a strong person. You'll be okay. You'll make it." And here's where I say, "No, I don't feel very strong right now and I'm not so sure I'm going to be okay."

When my husband passed away, I thought, "I'll never laugh again. There's nothing to laugh about or be joyful for anymore." But I can remember the first time I laughed out loud after losing my husband. It was simply a comical commercial on TV with a cow. I don't remember what they were promoting, I just remember it was so funny and I could not help but laugh and I remember saying out loud, "Oh, I just laughed!" I thanked the Lord that I laughed but turned around and cried because I did laugh, and I thought I really shouldn't have done that. Doesn't seem to make any sense, does it? And no, it's not wrong to laugh. But there are so many emotions stirring in our minds when we lose the one we've been with for ___ years. (It was 51 years for me).

There's a particular verse that has come to mean so much to me. I call it my theme verse for my grieving journey. It's John 10:10 "The thief cometh not but to steal, to kill and destroy. I am come that you might have life and that you might have it more abundantly." So, my motto, so to speak, is this: **GRIEVE, YES—BUT LIVE WHILE YOU DO!**

As I think of all my different emotions, I remember going to church on Sunday mornings and when certain hymns or choruses were sung, I would totally lose it. Tears would be shed as I thought about how some of them were Autry's favorites. And for some reason, Sunday evening services and Wednesday night prayer meetings were hard for me, and I would hurry out as fast as I could before the tears would stream down my face; sometimes making it even hard to see to drive home to that empty apartment. Often, I would just sit in my car, with tears still streaming down my cheeks, looking into the heavens, knowing he was up there somewhere. Oh, how I missed him!

And then there were those times when there were "triggers," and out of the blue, tears would come. I cried in a bank and at a post office. Tellers and counter workers would ask about my husband, not knowing he was gone, and I would just start crying. The first time I had a sub for lunch, I ended up crying because it reminded me how much he liked them. My sister-in-law and I went for lunch at Olive Garden, and I hardly got seated and looked around and saw other couples together and started crying as this was one of our favorite lunch places. Coming home from grocery shopping was another thing that brought tears as he always helped me put things away. And, of course, when I didn't feel good, it was harder because there was no one to take care of me; no one to just give me a hug! One more grueling thing I had to do as a widow was fill out various forms, etc. after his death and must check the "widow's box!" I still find that hard to do.

I kept a box with the cards and notes people sent me after his death. I was surprised that for several weeks afterward, I would still receive a card with a note saying how they were praying for me. That meant so much to me. But after a while the cards stopped coming, the visits were fewer, the phone calls were fewer. That's when I realized I needed to be careful. I knew self-pity and depression could so easily take over my life. I could have just stayed in bed, sat in the house, curled up in a chair, and forgot the rest of the world. Some days I didn't want to get up. I could have drowned in my grief. Please don't get me wrong; there is nothing wrong with grieving. We need to grieve, and we need to grieve for as long as it takes. But at the same time, we can live! Here's my verse again: **John 10:10 "I am come that they might have life, and that they might have it more abundantly."**

Although people were important to be around and they gave me much support, I realized my biggest support was going to come from God Himself and that meant there were some choices I had to make. I chose to have a deep dependence on God rather than live a life of despair; I chose to be filled with God's presence and accept all that God was doing in my life and what He wanted me to do, rather than be filled with self-pity and problems.

I needed to accept the fact that God is in control of all things. Rom. 8:28 "For we know that all things work together for good to them that love God, to them who are the called according to His purpose." I realized that not all things ARE good, but all things work together FOR good; that included all things in my life, and part of that had to do with my Autry. I was married at one point and now He has me single, as a widow.

I found the following verse to be one of the most instructive portions of scripture about trusting God:

Isa. 26:3-4 *"Thou will keep him in perfect peace whose mind is stayed on thee because he trusts in you. Trust ye in the Lord forever, for in the Lord Jehovah is everlasting strength."*

The **KEY** to peace when we are flooded with grief is to **KEEP OUR MIND FIXED ON THE LORD.** So, it's a promise, but with a condition! He will give us peace if we keep our mind focused or fixed on the Lord rather than be consumed with our grief. (Yes, we can grieve, but we can also live!). I can't stress enough the need to be in God's word when we have suffered a loss. I found myself in the Book of Psalms the most. There was so much comfort in that book.

After my husband passed away, I just needed to feel God's presence, and I did feel his presence the most when I had my devotions in my sunroom, which I started calling "My SON room." There was one morning in particular that I was feeling rather down and as I sat on the couch reading God's word, with the blinds open behind me; the sun started to come up and the rays of sunshine entered the room. I could feel the warmth on my shoulders. Till this day, I feel it was God giving me that hug I needed so desperately that morning.

The more I read and the more I studied, the more I was assured that this great God, who had saved me and lives within me, was not going to forsake me or leave me alone. He was going to be my comforter, my protector, my provider, my peace, my refuge, my encouragement, my all! I was in His sovereign hands. I could trust Him. I could trust His word because Jesus never fails! I can't stress enough the need to be in God's word when we have suffered a loss. Don't let Satan play games with your mind. Claim the truths that are in God's word to counter any lies that Satan tries to tell you.

A lot of questions flooded my mind after my loss. Probably the biggest one was "What now; how am I going to make it?" And God reminded me of another portion of scripture, which is read mostly at funerals, but has so much encouragement in it for all believers, and I think especially for those who are mourning. It's known as the Shepherd Psalm – Psalm 23. I love the thought of a shepherd himself; how he cares for his sheep, he knows their name, he protects, wards off predators, carries the weak and searches for any strays. How like this is our precious Shepherd, the Lord Jesus Christ! I'm so thankful He calls me one of His sheep. He knows my name, and as I read down through this precious Psalm, I realize He is my comforter, my protector, my defender, my guide. He is all powerful and all-knowing and He will provide all I need. I can trust Him with all my fears about the future, money, getting sick, being alone and so much more.

The main thing I need to ask myself is, "Who am I going to trust? Myself? My feelings? Or God?" The answer must be God. And when I say that I do not need to fear or worry. He is my Shepherd!

I knew the holidays would never be the same again. I always tried to be with some family members or friends although it didn't always happen. I think early on, I was almost afraid to talk about my husband, but since then I've found it's important to be able to talk about him. After all he was an important part of my life and of my family. There are still some old traditions that work for me; but I'm finding it's all right to start new ones.

I felt the second year was harder for me than the first, and I've heard many others say the same thing. I think it's because that first year you are so numb from everything, and you have so much to do and take care of that perhaps you didn't have to before. It's a whole new learning process of just discovering who you are now.

There are so many **dark clouds** you go through on the grieving journey, but remembering that we are not alone and that we have Someone who walks with us, Someone who knows all about us, Someone who cares and loves us more than anyone else. We can, with God's help, **break through those clouds of darkness into the light** and truly live again as God wants us to live.

BE STILL AND.....

> The more I read and the more I studied, the more I was assured that this great God, who had saved me and lives within me, was not going to forsake me or leave me alone. He was going to be my comfort, my protector, my provider, my peace, my refuge, my encouragement, my all! I was in His sovereign hands. I could trust Him.

READ THE WORD

"Thou will keep him in perfect peace whose mind is stayed on thee because he trusts in you. Trust ye in the Lord forever, for in the Lord Jehovah is everlasting strength."
Isa. 26:3-4

HIDE THE WORD

"The thief comes to steal, and to kill, and to destroy; I am come that you might have life and that you might have it more abundantly"
John 10:10

PRAY THE WORD

Dear Father, Guard my thoughts while I am on this journey of grief. Satan is trying to steal peace and joy from me; but You have given me life and you want me to live it abundantly. Help me to keep my mind fixed on you and to trust you; for you are my strength. Amen

KNOW THAT I AM GOD

Psalm 46:10

THE YEAR – 2020!

So, my journey up to this point had taken me through a lot of storms: storms of grief, storms of pain, storms of uncertainty. But as He had in the past, He would once again take me through some more dark clouds forming on the horizon.

Totally **unexpected storm clouds** in our lives can arise in a moment's time. We're often not prepared to hear the life-threatening news. It can throw us into complete despair or throw us to our knees. This is why staying in a right relationship with the Lord is so important and knowing what His word says so we can lean on its truths. (See my beginning chapters). Truths such as:

All things work together for good…
I can call upon God and He WILL hear me.
What time I am afraid I can trust in Him.
God is my refuge and my strength.
My hope is in Him.
My time is in His hands.

How can any of us forget the year 2020 as we were hit with Covid and everything that went along with it? It was a very difficult year for me for several reasons. Early in the year, I was diagnosed with esophagitis and acid reflux. Because my mom had passed away at 71 with a massive heart attack, my doctor ordered several tests on my heart (because of all the discomfort in my chest) just to see if anything was going on. All tests came back negative.

SO WHY DID THIS HAPPEN?

June 9, 2020, started out as a beautiful Saturday. At noon I met with some people in our church parking lot where we each enjoyed our own lunch and fellowshipped under the shade of a tall tree. Sprinkles started to come as the sky darkened, thunder rumbled in the distance, and we all left for our homes.

At home, I realized my kitchen window needed to be closed as rain was already coming in. However, the crank wouldn't close the window tightly and I needed to push it in from the outside. As I opened the door and had one leg out on the steps I started to fall back into the kitchen. It almost felt that a few seconds stopped, and I was falling in slow motion.

LET ME STOP HERE FOR YOU TO UNDERSTAND HOW GOD WATCHED OVER ME THAT DAY.

I had a couple (Matt and Rhonda) living in my basement at that time. God had brought them to me in a unique way. They also had a dog named Lily. That day the couple was supposed to go away, but situations came up and they stayed home. Lily needed to go potty three times, but because of rain and thunder she wouldn't go out—that is until the third time. At the same time, I headed out my kitchen door and I started to fall; Matt had Lily at the sunroom door. I saw him and was able to call for help as I was falling back inside onto the floor. I lay on the floor for some time with both Matt and Rhonda beside me. I did not want to move too quickly, as I thought since I had two hip replacements and both shoulders repaired, I might have done some damage to something. I was feeling slight discomfort in my chest but passed it off for acid reflux; after all, the tests were fine!

After finally getting up and talking to my daughter over the phone, we decided I should go to the ER just to check things out. Since there were visitor restrictions, I could not have anyone come in with me. I registered rather quickly and after they heard I was having some chest discomfort; I was rushed to the back. It wasn't very long before a doctor came in and told me I'd had a heart attack!

Really? The Nitro pills they gave me were not helping. The pain had become worse, and I was placed in ICU in the middle of the night with a nitro drip to keep me stable. The following day (Sunday) after having a covid test, I was taken by ambulance to a hospital in Rochester, NY. Monday morning, they performed a catheterization. I thought maybe they would have to put some stents in my heart, but when I came out of sedation, I was informed they could not do this; the blockages were too bad. I needed open heart surgery. The next morning (Tuesday) the operation took place; open heart surgery (a quadruple bypass)! I was in the hospital for a week with no one able to come to see me. My children were so upset they couldn't be with me. This was probably one of the loneliest and hardest times I had ever gone through.

I called this whole event a miracle. I shouldn't be here. I wouldn't be here; but God used four things to get me to the hospital because I wouldn't have gone if I had been by myself. After all, I was healthy. It couldn't be my heart—right?

BUT GOD USED:

- A couple who was supposed to be away; but was home
- A thunderstorm
- A doggie that had to go potty 3 times, but wouldn't go out until the "right time"
- A fall

Coincidence? Not in my book! What an awesome God we have!

Here I am, recovered from surgery and life goes on. Sure, there are some things that I can't do like I used to be able to do, and it may take me a little longer to do those things that I can do. But my life has found a "new normal," and God continues to bless me as He always has. He has opened other avenues of ministry for me as I prayed and asked Him to show me what He still wants me to do. I have become a co-leader for our Grief Share program at church and more recently became co-leader for a widow's and single's ladies community group in my home in which I teach our Bible Study. Speaking engagements come up now and then, and I continue to post a blog each Monday morning on my website (marleneburling.com).

God spared my life, apparently for a reason. My desire is that the remaining days of my life (however long they may be) will be used for His glory and honor. There is an old hymn that expresses what I want my life to be:

Only One Life

Avis B. Christiansen

Only one life to offer—Jesus, my Lord and King;
Only one tongue to praise Thee and of Thy mercy sing.
Only one heart's devotion—Savior, O may it be
Consecrated alone to Thy matchless glory, Yielded fully to Thee.

Only this hour is mine, Lord—May it be used for Thee;
May ev'ry passing moment Count for eternity.
Souls all about are dying, Dying in sin and shame.
Help me bring them the message of Calv'ry's
redemption In Thy glorious name.

Only one life to offer—Take it, dear Lord, I pray;
Nothing from Thee with holding, Thy will I now obey.
Thou who hast freely given Thine all in all for me,
Claim this life for Thine own to be used, my
Savior, Ev'ry moment for Thee."

BE STILL AND.....

> Totally unexpected storm clouds in our lives can arise in a moment's time. We're often not prepared to hear the life-threatening news. It can throw us into complete despair or throw us to our knees.

READ THE WORD

"Why are you cast down, O my soul? And why are you disquieted within me? Hope in God: for I shall yet praise him, who is the health of my countenance, and my God.
Psalm 42:11

HIDE THE WORD

"And we know that all things work together for good to them that love God, to them who are the called according to his purpose."
Rom. 8:28

PRAY THE WORD

Dear Father, Help me to realize that I may not understand why all the storm clouds arise in my life; but that you have a reason and a purpose for them. Help me not to be in despair, but rather praise you instead for you are my hope and my God. Amen

KNOW THAT I AM GOD

Psalm 46:10

MY DESIRE – TO FINISH WELL

There will always be clouds that we need to break through all the days of our lives. We can expect that to be so. But we can also prepare our hearts spiritually and arm ourselves with the Word of God so when those dark clouds surround us, we can break through them with the Lord's help. We are victors in Him.

Gal 2:20 continues to be so much encouragement to me: "I am crucified with Christ: nevertheless I live; yet not I, but Christ lives in me: and the life which I now live in the flesh I live by the faith of the Son of God, who loved me, and gave himself for me." Knowing that He lives IN me and that He is always faithful and that He never fails, gives me the hope I need to live every day of my life.

He is Elohim – the strong, faithful One! I can "Be still and know that He is God."

When I first became a Christian in April of 1967, there was a song that became special to me. It was called, "I Just Want to Count for God." I chose that title to be my "motto" throughout my life. That was my heart's desire; I wanted God to use me until He takes me home. I just want to finish well.

I'm going to leave you with a few more verses that are particularly special to me now in this stage of my life.

> ➤ *"The days of our years are threescore years and ten: and if by reason of strength they be fourscore years, yet is their strength*

labor and sorrow; for it is soon cut off, and we fly away" Psalm 90:10, 12.
- *"The steps of a good man are ordered by the LORD: and he delights in his way." Psalm 37:23.*
- *"That I may publish with the voice of thanksgiving and tell of all thy wondrous works" Psalm 26:7.*
- *"But I will hope continually, and will yet praise thee more and more. My mouth shall show forth thy righteousness and thy salvation all the day; for I know not the numbers thereof. I will go in the strength of the Lord GOD: I will make mention of thy righteousness, even of You only. O God; thou hast taught me from my youth: and up to now I have declared thy wondrous works. Now also when I am old and gray headed, O God, forsake me not; until I have shown thy strength unto this generation, and thy power to everyone that is to come." Psalm 71:14-18*

Breaking through the clouds is not something you can do on your own. But no matter how dark those clouds may be that you are going through at this moment, trust God. He will bring you through to the other side, in His time, where the SON is shining!

BE STILL AND.....

> There will always be clouds that we need to break through all the days of our lives. We can expect that to be so. But we can also prepare our hearts spiritually and arm ourselves with the Word of God

READ THE WORD

"But I will hope continually, and will yet praise thee more and more. My mouth shall show forth thy righteousness and thy salvation all the day; for I know not the numbers thereof. I will go in the strength of the Lord GOD: I will make mention of thy righteousness, even of You only. O God; thou hast taught me from my youth: and up to now I have declared thy wondrous works. Now also when I am old and gray headed, O God, forsake me not; until I have shown thy strength unto this generation, and thy power to everyone that is to come."
Psalm 71:14-18

HIDE THE WORD

"That I may publish with the voice of thanksgiving, and tell of all thy wondrous works."
Psalm 26:7

PRAY THE WORD

Dear Father, You know my heart's desire is "to end well." I ask that You give me the strength to continue to serve you all the days of my life and that I can share with the world all the things that You have brought me through and taught me along the way. So, even in my "older age" use me to bring glory and honor to your name. I love you. Amen.

KNOW THAT I AM GOD

Psalm 46:10

ABOUT THE AUTHOR

Marlene Burling is a widow, a resident of Batavia, NY. She was a pastor's wife, married for 51 years. She has 3 children, 10 grandchildren and 10 great grandchildren. Their ministry began in home missions and later transitioned to regular pastorates. She has been a teacher of children, youth, and ladies, and is presently a speaker for ladies' events.

Her writing began after the loss of her husband. She has written a children's book, "Grandma, Tell Me the Easter Story," and two 365-day devotionals; "Morning Walks with God," and "A Daily Walk with God." She writes a weekly inspirational blog on Monday mornings on her website (marleneburling.com) and on her face book page (under Marlene L. Burling) the other days of the week.

She has developed a workshop for widows and others who have suffered the loss of a loved one, which is titled, "There's Life after Loss," which she has presented at two ladies' state conferences, some churches and at a special presentation and book signing at a bookstore. She is the co-leader of "Grief Share," at her church, Grace Baptist Church in Batavia, NY, and is also co-leader for a ladies' single's and widow's community group which meets in her home where she leads their Bible study.

God has taken Marlene through many times of loss, pain, and grief as well as disappointments and heartaches. Her desire for this book is that as she shares what God has done in her life, it will be an encouragement and help to those experiencing similar situations. John 10:10 continues to be her theme verse, as it was in her devotionals. ***"The thief comes to steal, kill, and destroy; I am come that you might have life; and that you might have it more abundantly."*** Satan is always trying to destroy our relationship with our Lord, but Jesus is greater than he and Jesus is the one who can help us **"break through any cloud"** that may be surrounding us and give us that abundant life that he wants us to live.

www.ingramcontent.com/pod-product-compliance
Lightning Source LLC
LaVergne TN
LVHW011717060526
838200LV00051B/2934